Mary With Us

Mary With Us

Readings and Prayers

Rev. Joseph A. Viano, SSP

ALBA · HOUSE   NEW · YORK

SOCIETY OF ST. PAUL, 2187 VICTORY BLVD., STATEN ISLAND, NEW YORK 10314

ACKNOWLEDGMENTS

Mary, Mother and Model by James Alberione, S.S.P. — *Daily Reflections*.
St. Paul Editions (Daughters of St. Paul) Boston.

Queen of Heaven. The Leaflet Missal Company. St. Paul, Minn.

Illustrations by Sr. Anjelica Ballan. of the Pious Disciples of the
Divine Master, Rome.

Rev. Joseph A. Viano, S.S.P.
Mary With Us
ISBN: 0-8189-0559-X

Imprimi Potest:
Rev. Edmund Lane, S.S.P.
Censor Delegatus
Society of St. Paul

Imprimatur:
† Most Rev. James W. Malone
Bishop of Youngstown, Ohio

Nihil Obstat:
Rev. James A. Clarke. Chancellor
Censor
October 31, 1988

Designed, printed and bound in the United States of
America by the Fathers and Brothers of the
Society of St. Paul, 2187 Victory Boulevard,
Staten Island. New York 10314, as part of their
communications apostolate.

Printing Information:

Current Printing - first digit   2 3 4 5 6 7 8 9 10 11 12

Year of Current Printing - first year shown

1993   1994   1995   1996

FOREWORD

Devotion to Mary is as old as the Church itself. Her whole life, from the time we meet her in the pages of Sacred Scripture when the angel told her that she was to become the Mother of the Son of God, through the birth and boyhood of Jesus, the beginning of His public life at the marriage feast of Cana, His passion and death on Calvary, His resurrection and ascension into heaven, and the descent of His Holy Spirit upon her and the disciples at Pentecost, has been a source of inspiration to countless millions.

Through the pages of this book you will read that Mary received, from an angel, the great message of the Incarnation, and she receives, now, God's mesages and communicated them to us and to the world. Mary is honored on earth with the most beautiful Prayers and Devotions: by saying these prayers and practicing these devotions we will receive a great abundance of heavenly favors, graces and blessings.

In each chapter of this book, priests will find a mini-meditation, and good material for a short sermon on Mary.

It is hoped that the sentiments expressed here will lead the reader to a deeper appreciation of the role of Mary in our lives and to a greater love for Jesus, her Divine Son.

— Rev. Edmund Lane, S.S.P.

"By the will of God, the most Blessed Virgin Mary was inseparably joined with Christ in accomplishing the work of man's redemption, so that our salvation flows from the love of Jesus Christ and His sufferings intimately united with the love and sorrows of His Mother. It is, then, highly fitting that, after due homage has been paid to the most Sacred Heart of Jesus, Christian people, who have obtained divine life from Christ through Mary, manifest similar piety and the love of their grateful souls for the most loving heart of our heavenly Mother."

Pope John XXIII

CONTENTS

Prayer. — To you, O Mary, we give our bodies, our hearts, and our souls; to you we give our homes, our families, our country. We desire that all that is in us and around us may share in the benefits of your motherly affections and care.

Mary . . . Christ . . .

Mary the dawn, Christ the perfect day;
Mary the gate, Christ the heavenly way.
Mary the root, Christ the mystic vine;
Mary the grape, Christ the sacred wine.
Mary the wheat, Christ the living bread;
Mary the stem, Christ the rose: blood-red.
Mary the font, Christ the cleansing flood;
Mary the chalice, Christ the saving blood.
Mary the temple, Christ the temple's Lord;
Mary the shrine, Christ the God adored.
Mary the beacon, Christ the haven's rest;
Mary the mirror, Christ the vision blest.
Mary the Mother, Christ the Mother's Son;
By all things blest while endless ages run.

PART ONE — THE MOST BEAUTIFUL AND POPULAR PRAYERS AND HYMNS IN HONOR OF MARY

THE HAIL MARY

Universally recognized as the most beautiful prayer said in honor of Our Lady, The *Hail Mary* is a combination of the words said by the Archangel Gabriel at the Annunciation, and the words of Elizabeth at the Visitation. The second part consists of words of petition, added by the Church.

Hail Mary, full of grace, the Lord is with you, Blessed are you among women and blessed is the fruit of your womb, Jesus. Holy Mary, Mother of God, pray for us sinners, now and at the hour of our death. — Amen.

St. Louis de Montfort said: ''The *Hail Mary* is the most beautiful compliment we can pay to Mary because God, to conquer her heart, first offered it to her through an angel. The Hail Mary is a heavenly dew which sprinkles the dry and sterile soul until it bears fruit at an opportune time . . . The *Hail Mary* is the hammer which crushes the devil and is the joy of the angels, the melody of the predestined, and the canticle of the New Testament . . . .

The *Hail Mary* is a chaste and loving kiss that we give to Mary, a brilliant red rose we offer to her, a precious pearl we present to her . . . . It is a divine flower gathered by an archangel in heavenly gardens and shown to us so that we will offer it to Mary.''

St. Bonaventure prayed: "O Mary, you are full of grace! But what am I saying? You have grace in superabundance, and every soul lives of this superabundance communicated to the world."

THE "THREE HAIL MARYS" DEVOTION

The devotion of *Three Hail Marys* goes back to the 13th Century, and is also called "A Little Key of Heaven" devotion.

Saint Matilde, a Benedictine nun from Hacheborn, Germany, was very devoted to Mary, and was favored with many visions from her. During one of the visions, Matilde opened her heart to Mary, complaining that she was worrying about her last hours and was afraid of losing her soul. She asked for Mary's special assistance at that supreme moment. Smiling, Our Blessed Mother promised to help her if she did something very simple to honor her during the remainder of her life. "See, daughter," Mary said, "I have a little key that will open the door of heaven for you when you die. All you have to do is to say, in my honor, three Hail Marys every day."

Matilde practiced this devotion faithfully, every day, and died a very happy death, assisted by Mary.

The devotion of the three Hail Marys every day, morning and night, was my very first devotion toward Mary. I had hardly learned to say this prayer, when I started hearing my mother shouting from the first floor: "Hey, boys (there were six of us) do not forget to say the three Hail Marys!"

Among the saints who constantly practiced and encouraged the devotion of the Three Hail Marys were

St. Anthony of Padua, who declared that the aim of this practice is "to honor the spotless Virginity of Mary and to preserve a perfect purity of mind, heart and body." St. Leonard of Port-Maurice said that the purpose of this devotion is "to honor Mary Immaculate and to obtain the grace of avoiding all mortal sins during the day or night." St. Alphonsus de Liguori earnestly recommended this devotion "to the devout and to sinners, to the young and old."

For Mary's protection during day and night, and to obtain a happy death at the end of our lives, let us practice this very simple devotion with faithfulness. You can simply say three Hail Marys at the beginning of every new day, while dressing and getting ready to face the various activities of the day, and again (if you wish), at night, while undressing and getting ready to go to bed.

If you desire to make this devotion more *formal,* I suggest that you set apart a convenient time in the morning and at night just for that.

In the morning, make the Sign of the Cross, say devoutly three Hail Marys, and, if you wish, follow this pattern:

MORNING OFFERING

Divine Heart of Jesus, I offer you, through the Immaculate Heart of Mary, Mother of the Church, in union with the Eucharistic Sacrifice: my prayers, actions, joys and sufferings of this day, in reparation for sins and for the salvation of all mankind, in the grace of the Holy Spirit, for the glory of the heavenly Father.

TO SPEND THE DAY WELL

My dear and sweet Mother Mary, keep your holy hand upon my head; guard my mind, my heart and my senses, that I may never commit sin. Sanctify my thoughts, affections, words and actions, so that I may please you and your Jesus, my God, and reach heaven with you. Jesus and Mary, give me your holy blessing: in the name of the Father, and of the Son, and of the Holy Spirit. Amen.

In the evening: make the Sign of the Cross, say three Hail Marys again, and add these invocations:

Jesus, Mary and Joseph, I give you my heart and my soul.

Jesus, Mary and Joseph, assist me in my last agony.

Jesus, Mary and Joseph, may I breathe forth my soul in peace with you.

(These prayers of the Three Hail Marys Devotion could replace the Morning and Evening Prayers).

* * *

A STORY: "HERE LIVES A FREETHINKER" — On May 17, 1926, a priest wrote from Namur — "I was curate of . . . . In this city lived a man who placed a sign over his door which read: 'Here lives a freethinker.'

"This man became seriously ill and was in danger of death. In spite of the sign over the freethinker's door, being the curate, having a responsibility for this soul, I knocked on the door. Upon seeing me, the dying man cried out violently:

" 'My rifle, my rifle, give me my rifle!' " In fact a rifle was hanging over his bed.

" 'It matters little, my friend,' " I answered. " 'You want your rifle and I shall give it to you' ". . . .

" 'Ah, you are not afraid,' " he added with surprise. " 'This astounds me.' "

" 'No, my friend, I am not afraid.' "

"He did not shoot. In fact, we soon began to chat a bit.

"After a few days the freethinker agreed to accept, as his nurse, his own sister, who was a Religious. One of the first tasks of that holy soul was to remove the famous sign from his door. Not long after I was able to administer the Sacraments to the sick man. After this, surprised at my success, I said to him:

" 'Well, you are fortunate. All your life you have been a rascal. You did all the harm you could possibly do in this life; nevertheless, you are going to Heaven!' "

" 'I hope so,' " he answered.

Then I asked him to what he attributed such a great grace. He answered frankly:

" 'To the Blessed Virgin. On the day of my First Communion, I promised to recite my three Hail Marys daily, and I never failed. This was my only religious practice.' "

A PRAYER — O Mary, dearly beloved Mother, how close to God you are and how utterly filled with Him! Obtain for me the grace of loving my Jesus; obtain for me the grace of loving you.

THE SALVE REGINA

The *Salve Regina* was probably written by Hermanus or St. Bernard of Clairvaux (12th Century). Used as a conclusion of the Breviary recitation and during religious processions, the Hail Holy Queen is a prayer of celebrating the Queenship of Mary, Mother of Mercy. When we say this beautiful prayer, we consider ourselves as pilgrims, asking Mary to assist and protect us during our earthly pilgrimage, obtain for us a happy death, and lead us to eternal salvation.

Hail holy Queen, Mother of mercy, our life, our sweetness and our hope. To you do we cry, poor banished children of Eve; to you do we send up our sighs, mourning and weeping in this valley of tears. Turn then, most gracious advocate, your eyes of mercy toward us; and after this our exile, show to us the blessed fruit of your womb, Jesus. O clement, O loving, O sweet Virgin Mary.

St. Alphonsus de Liguori wrote: "As the glorious Virgin Mary has been raised to the dignity of Mother of the King of Kings, it is not without reason that the Church honors her, and wishes her to be honored by all, with the glorious title of *Queen.* Queen so sweet, clement, and so ready to help us in our miseries, that the holy Church wills that we should salute her in this prayer under the title of Queen of Mercy."

St. Bernard asks why the Church calls Mary "The Queen of Mercy"? And he replies that, "it is because we believe that she opens the abyss of the Mercy of God to whomsoever she wills, when she wills, and as she wills; so that there is no sinner, however great, who is lost if Mary protects him."

PRAYER TO THE BLESSED VIRGIN TO OBTAIN A GOOD DEATH

Mary, my sweet mother, refuge of sinners, when my soul is on the point of leaving this world assist me with the same sorrow and compassion with which you assisted your son on the cross. Drive from me the evil enemy, take me to yourself and present me to the eternal Judge. My Queen, do not abandon me. After Jesus, you will to be my comfort at the moment of death. Beg your beloved Son, in his goodness, to grant me the grace to die clinging to your feet and to breathe forth my soul into his wounds, saying, "Jesus and Mary, I give you my heart and my soul." Amen.

— *St. Alphonsus de Liguori.*

A Story: Lifted Up Towards Mary's Picture. — St. Alphonsus de Liguori, the great Marian Doctor of the Church, the singer of Mary's divine glories, is the fervent apostle of a tender and trusting devotion to her.

In his well known classic book "The Glories of Mary," he gave us the most complete and the most beautiful commentary on the "Hail Holy Queen" prayer.

Alphonsus was born of noble and pious parents near Naples, on September 27, 1696. A few days later he was baptized at the Church of Mary Most Holy of the Virgins, and was placed under her special protection.

His was the singular grace of being brought up by a saintly mother, who instilled in him a tender piety and a great love for Mary Most Holy. Every day Alphonsus prayed to Mary in a transport of delight; he called her his Mother, his Protectress and his Hope. This most charming flower of Mary's garden did not delay long in showing its fruits. He grew in age and in sanctity, and in the midst of grave perils, preserved his baptismal innocence intact.

Deeming himself unworthy of the high dignity of the priesthood, Alphonsus undertook a career in law, and in a short time became one of the most outstanding lawyers. This was not his vocation, however; Mary wanted him to become a priest, an apostle.

When he inadvertently compromised a lawsuit, he was so deeply moved that he decided to abandon law.

Hearing the Lord's call to join His followers, he answered promptly. He overcame the obstacles that were placed in his path by his relatives, and devoted himself to sacred studies with great love. In preparation for the priesthood, he resolved to fast every Saturday in honor of Mary Most Holy, and Mary formed him into a perfect priest and apostle.

His priestly life was the life of a true apostle, of a sincere lover of Jesus and Mary. His favorite topic for sermons was the Blessed Mother, and with these, he obtained the most striking conversions.

One day, while he was preaching the Novena of the Assumption on the coasts of Amalfi, he said, "Behold, I am going to pray to Mary for you all, but you ask graces for me, too, in this moment." There was fire in those words. He became radiant, then was lifted upwards over the pulpit toward a picture of the Blessed Virgin. And from this picture, a shaft of light enveloped him.

He was made Bishop of St. Agatha dei Goti, and the good he worked was immense. He wrote one hundred and twenty moral and spiritual works, which are permeated with the sublimest Marian sentiment. In "The Glories of Mary" he compiled the most solid doctrine of the Fathers and Doctors on Mary's privileges, goodness and protection.

Alphonsus died on July 31, 1787, at the ringing of the *Angelus,* assisted by the Blessed Virgin.

A Prayer. — O Blessed Virgin, Mother of God, from the depths of my heart I praise and extol you as the purest, the fairest, the holiest creature of all God's handiwork.

THE ANGELUS

The Angelus is a devotion practiced by many people at 6:00 A.M., 12 noon, and 6:00 P.M. This devotional practice commemorates the beginning of the history of our Redemption (Annunciation), and the Incarnation of Jesus in the womb of Mary, through the work of the Holy Spirit. Versicles referring to Mary and the Incarnation are used, with the recitation of three Hail Marys. This devotion is concluded with a prayer of intercession followed by the Glory be to the Father . . . . , in honor of the Blessed Trinity. It has been widely used by monks since the 11th century, and encouraged by many Popes, who enriched it with many indulgences.

THE ANGEL OF THE LORD
a) During the year (outside of Paschal Season)

V. The Angel of the Lord declared unto Mary,
R. And she conceived of the Holy Spirit.
Hail Mary.
V. Behold the handmaid of the Lord.
R. Be it done unto me according to your word.
Hail Mary.
V. And the Word was made flesh,
R. And dwelt among us.
Hail Mary.
V. Pray for us, O holy Mother of God,
R. That we may be made worthy of the promises of Christ.

Let us pray. — Pour forth, we beg you, O Lord, your grace into our hearts: that we, to whom the Incarnation of Christ your Son was made known by the message of an Angel, may by his Passion and cross be brought to the glory of his Resurrection. Through the same Christ our Lord. Amen.

* * *

b) During Paschal Season

Queen of Heaven, rejoice, alleluia:
For he whom you merited to bear, alleluia.
Has risen, as he said, alleluia.
Pray for us to God, alleluia.
V. Rejoice and be glad, O Virgin Mary, alleluia.
R. Because the Lord is truly risen, alleluia.
Let us pray. — O God, who by the Resurrection of your Son, our Lord Jesus Christ, granted joy to the whole world: grant, we beg you, that through the intercession of the Virgin Mary, his Mother, we may lay hold of the joys of eternal life. Through the same Christ our Lord. — *Amen.*

The Ven. James Alberione said: "Let us not seek comfort in creatures: they very often do nothing but increase our sorrow. Let us go to Mary, and we shall always find the merciful Mother who consoles and comforts . . . . The world must return to Jesus through Mary. The world must refer to the Church, to Jesus Christ, to His Vicar — through Mary. When devotion to Mary is a deep part of a soul, and when devotion to Mary becomes a part of the world, then there will be a transformation — a transformation that is spiritual, intellectual and a life-force."

A Story: St. Pius X and the Angelus. — The entire life of this august Pontiff was a hymn of faith and love to Jesus in the Holy Eucharist and to the Blessed Virgin. He was born in Riese on June 2, 1835, and the following day was baptized Joseph.

As a boy Joseph used to go often to the Shrine of *Maria delle Cendrole,* and on Sundays he would bring his friends along. There he would pray devoutly. The Madonna called him to the priesthood, but his parents were poor and could not pay for his studies. Providentially the Patriarch of Venice intervened and granted the boy a scholarship. After his ordination to the priesthood, Joseph was appointed a curate in Tombolo, in the diocese of Treviso, where he put his zeal for souls into action.

In 1875 he was elected a Canon of the Cathedral of Treviso and in 1884 Leo XIII consecrated him Bishop of Mantua. The fame of the Bishop of Mantua's wisdom and piety grew steadily, and Leo XIII made him a Cardinal and then Patriarch of Venice.

In 1903, the renowned Patriarch of Venice, Cardinal Sarto, was elected Pope and he took the name of Pius X. The more promotions he received, the greater became his manifestation of love for Jesus in the Holy Eucharist and Mary Immaculate. On the occasion of the fiftieth anniversary of the dogma of the Immaculate Conception, Pius X wrote an encyclical on the Madonna: *"Ad diem illum,"* the masterpiece of his devotion to Mary. He describes Mary Most Holy's beauty, her virginity and her influence on humanity; he urges all Christians to be devoted to this good Mother.

One day during an audience granted to some noblemen of Rome, he heard the Angelus ring. At once, he said, "Gentlemen, it is the hour of the Angelus. Will you recite it with me?" An eyewitness described him as follows: "I observed him while he prayed. I contemplated the expression on his face, the radiant light in his eyes as he gazed steadily at a picture of the Blessed Virgin. I admired the sweetness of those 'Hail Marys' said in such an unusual tone. I was so vividly impressed that I was forced to think: 'Perhaps he sees her.' And I realized then how much we must love the Mother of God."

St. Pius X died on August 20, 1914.

Prayer. — Most glorious Virgin, chosen by God to be the Mother of the eternal Word made flesh, be my guide and counselor in this vale of tears.

THE MAGNIFICAT:

A Song of Praise and Thanksgiving

Mary's song of thanksgiving and praise for the mighty act that God has wrought in her and for the salvation that He has given to Israel, is set in the scene of Mary's Visitation to her cousin Elizabeth. This canticle was spoken by the Blessed Virgin Mary when greeted by Elizabeth, who recognized in her the blessed Mother of Our Lord, and is widely used by the priests and people at the conclusion of Vespers.

Mary's Canticle

My soul magnifies the Lord,
  and my spirit rejoices in God my Savior;
Because he has regarded the lowliness of his
  handmaid; for, behold, henceforth all
  generations shall call me blessed;
Because he who is mighty has done great
  things for me, and holy is his name;
And his mercy is from generation to generation
  on those who fear him.
He has shown might with his arm,
  he has scattered the proud in the conceit of
  their heart.
He has put the mighty from their thrones,
  and has exalted the lowly.
He has filled the hungry with good things,
  and the rich he has sent away empty.
He has given help to Israel, his servant,
  mindful of his mercy —
Even as he spoke to our fathers —
  to Abraham and to his posterity forever.

The Ven. James Alberione wrote these beautiful words about Mary: "O Mary, it is sweet to turn my first look upon you in the morning, to walk beneath your mantle during the day, or fall asleep under your gaze at night . . . . Through the grace of Baptism, Mary introduced us to the Christian life; through the grace of the Sacraments, she introduced us to a life of sanctity. With the grace of final perseverance, she will introduce us to eternal life . . . . Let us entrust our temporal and spiritual needs to Mary. If our necessities are great, Mary's power is also great; and if we ask with faith, we shall certainly receive."

A Story: Pius IX, the Pope of the Immaculate Conception. — The name of this Pontiff cannot be separated from the name of the Blessed Virgin Mary, to whom he was greatly devoted. In 1854, he solemnly proclaimed and defined, from the immovable rock of the Vatican, the dogma of Mary's Immaculate Conception — a dogma which, four years later, the Virgin herself deigned to confirm to the humble Bernadette Soubirous in the grotto of Massabielle.

Mary carried out a special mission in his regard. She protected him in the midst of every danger. She made him strong and fearless. She formed him after her own heart, instilling in him all those sentiments of charity, love and compassion by which a father, an apostle, and a saint must be inspired.

Born in times which were very sorrowful for the Church, and when it seemed as though the gates of hell would prevail, this future Pope entrusted himself to Mary from his earliest years. And the Blessed Virgin, who was watching over him, led him into the priesthood, helping him to overcome very great difficulties. In 1828, Pope Leo XII elected him Archbishop of Spoleto; Pope Gregory XVI, admiring his zeal and sanctity, transferred him to Imola so that there, too, he might restore the state of the Church as he had done in Spoleto. In a short time these two dioceses rose to a new life and splendor. His pastoral activities in these two dioceses were such that he was believed to be another St. Charles Borromeo or another St. Francis, and some, upon seeing him, exclaimed, "There goes our future Pope." And they were not mistaken.

His superior gifts and tireless zeal so impressed Gregory XVI that he made him a Cardinal in 1839. He was then forty-eight. A few years later he ascended the throne of Peter.

Finally he was able to make known to the whole world his filial affection for the Blessed Virgin; at last the time had arrived to declare as an article of faith that which Christians of all centuries had always believed: the Immaculate Conception of the Blessed Virgin Mary. He zealously sought to make devotion to the most holy Mother of God grow in men's hearts. He exhorted, encouraged and invited everyone by his own example to have recourse to Mary. And this ardent enthusiasm of his for devotion to Mary merited for him the singular protection of his heavenly Patroness. It was Mary who gave him strength and courage to withstand all persecutions, and when in 1848, the revolution forced him to flee to Gaeta, his sole comforts were the Holy Eucharist, which he carried with him, and his complete trust in Mary's powerful help.

On February 7, 1878, he took his flight to Heaven after exclaiming, ''Mother of mercy, protect us from our enemies and receive us in the hour of our death.''

Prayer. — Oh, holy Mary, convert me, and obtain for me the grace to love Jesus Christ above all things and to console you also by living a holy life, in order that one day I may be able to see you in Heaven.

THE MEMORARE

This short but beautiful prayer is attributed by some, to St. Augustine or St. John Chrysostom, but more surely to St. Bernard, who wrote so much and so beautifully about Our Lady. Claude Bernard, "the poor priest" of Paris (1588-1641) popularized and used this prayer extensively in his ministry. It is a prayer of full confidence in the goodness and sweetness of Mary, and the power of her intercession in every necessity of life.

The Memorare

Remember, O most gracious Virgin Mary, that never was it known that anyone who fled to your protection, implored your help or sought your intercession, was left unaided.

Inspired by this confidence, I fly to you, O Virgin of Virgins, my mother. To you I come; before you I stand, sinful and sorrowful.

O Mother of the Word Incarnate, despise not my petitions, but in your mercy, hear and answer me. Amen.

Ven. James Alberione, the founder of five Religious Congregations, and four Secular Institutes which constitute the "Pauline Family," wrote: "O Mary, it is sweet to turn my first look upon you in the morning, to walk beneath your mantle during the day, or fall asleep under your gaze at night . . . . Discouraged souls: turn to Mary! You sinners who feel your humiliation, turn to Mary! In doubts, in temptations, in daily encountered difficulties, in time of distrust, turn to Mary! Always to Mary. Call on Mary in every situation and refer to her in the way that a needy child looks to its mother and is sure of finding a Mother thinking of its concerns.''

A Story: ''Hail, Bernard!'' — St. Bernard was born in 1091 in Fontaines. He was the third of seven children and was consecrated to the Virgin Mary. When he was nineteen years of age, his mother died, and this young man then turned trustingly to his heavenly Mother and told her, ''You will be my mother.'' Mary indeed proved that she was his mother by protecting him from every danger, especially spiritual dangers.

Together with thirty other companions won by his enthusiastic words, he retired into the solitude of the Cistercian monastery. Here, in the silence of the cloister, Bernard's love for Mary increased greatly. He thought of her continually and sought to imitate her in her virtues. His every act, word and thought was directed to Mary. Such a great lover and affectionate, constant devotee of the Mother of God could not help but win her protection and benevolence. From his boyhood to his death, St. Bernard received continual and very special favors from the Blessed Virgin. During his stay at Chatillon, for example, he fell asleep while waiting in church at Christmas night. He then saw the mystery of the birth of Jesus exactly as it took place in the grotto of Bethlehem, and the Blessed Virgin, handing him the Holy Child said, ''Take, Bernard, my Son, the Redeemer of the world.''

On another occasion, in the year 1146, when he entered a church and greeted the Blessed Virgin three times, she replied three times: "Hail, Bernard." Likewise, when he hailed a statue of Mary with the words: "Hail, Mary," she deigned to answer him: "Hail, Bernard."

Consumed by hard work, fastings, watches, penance and his most austere way of life, Bernard bid farewell to his monks and dear ones on August 20, 1153, and became recollected in himself. A mysterious light flooded his cell, and Bernard sat up, stretched out his arms and smilingly said, "I am coming." The Blessed Virgin, whom he had loved so deeply, had come to take her beloved Bernard into the kingdom of glory.

Prayer. — Save me, O Mary, for you are my hope; save me from the pains of hell, but especially from sin, which alone has power to make me lose my soul.

WE FLY TO YOUR PATRONAGE

It is commonly believed that this is the most ancient prayer to Mary. We are under a continued stress; dangers surround us. We have only one place to fly for help and protection, under Mary's mantle.

We fly to your patronage, O holy Mother of God; despise not our petitions in our necessities, but deliver us always from all dangers, O glorious and blessed Virgin.

In distress and in every necessity, look to Mary!

Here are some of the most beautiful and comforting words of St. Bernard:

"O you who flounder amid the vicissitudes of life, as on the waves of a stormy sea, do not divert your eyes from Mary, Star of the Sea!

"If the winds of temptation blow about you, if your frail bark is hindered by the rocks of tribulations, look to the Star, invoke Mary!

"If anger or avarice or sensuality rock the tiny vessel of your heart, look at Mary!

"If you are troubled by the enormity of your sins and are on the verge of sliding into the abyss of discouragement, think of Mary!

"In dangers, in afflictions, in critical moments, remember Mary, call upon Mary!

"Never permit Mary's name to be far from your lips; may the thought of her be always fixed in your heart!

"By following her, you can never go astray; by praying to her you will never fall; by thinking of her you will never err; protected by her, you need not fear; guided by her, you will reach salvation.

"With Mary's protection, there is nothing to fear. Under her leadership, you will succeed. With her encouragement, all is possible."

A Story: Fra Bartholomew's Painting. — It was the year 1247. The Founders of the Servants of Mary in Florence entrusted to Fra Bartholomew, a distinguished and devout artist, the task of painting in their chapel a fresco depicting Mary in the act of receiving from the Archangel the annunciation of the Incarnation. The artist began the work at once. Soon the fresco neared completion; only the faces of the Blessed Virgin and the Angel remained to be painted.

The artist, however, felt incapable of giving expression to the great concept of the Annunciation. He attempted again and again in vain, until one day he fell asleep in utter discouragement. A few moments passed. Fra Bartholomew awoke, and beheld, to his great astonishment, the faces of the Blessed Virgin and the Angel beautifully painted and with heavenly expression. Beside himself with joy he cried out, "A miracle!" The Religious and the people came running, and stood in speechless admiration before those heavenly figures painted miraculously.

And this is the miraculous painting of the Annunciation in Florence, before which even in our day the faithful gather in devout prayer.

Prayer: Our most loving Mother, Treasurer of graces and Refuge of us poor sinners, we fly to your motherly affection with lively faith, certain that you will hear our prayers.

The Litany of the Blessed Virgin

Lord, have mercy on us.
Christ, have mercy on us.
Lord, have mercy on us.
Christ, hear us.
Christ, graciously hear us.
God, the Father of heaven,
have mercy on us.
God, the Son, Redeemer
of the world,
have mercy on us.
God, the Holy Spirit,
have mercy on us.
Holy Trinity, one God,
have mercy on us.

Holy Mary, *pray for us. . .*
Holy Mother of God,
Holy Virgin of Virgins,

Mother of Christ,
Mother of divine grace,
Mother most pure,
Mother most chaste,
Mother inviolate,
Mother undefiled,
Mother most amiable,
Mother most admirable,
Mother of good counsel,
Mother of our Creator,
Mother of our Savior,

Virgin most prudent,
Virgin most venerable,
Virgin most renowned,
Virgin most powerful,
Virgin most merciful,
Virgin most faithful,

Mirror of justice,
Seat of wisdom,
Cause of our joy,
Mystical rose,
Tower of David,
Tower of ivory,

House of gold,
Ark of the covenant,
Gate of heaven,
Morning star,
Health of the sick,
Refuge of sinners,
Comforter of the afflicted,
Help of Christians,

Queen of Angels,
Queen of Patriarchs,
Queen of Prophets,
Queen of Apostles,
Queen of Martyrs,
Queen of Confessors,
Queen of Virgins,
Queen of all Saints,
Queen conceived without
original sin,
Queen assumed into heaven,
Queen of the most holy Rosary,
Queen of peace,

Lamb of God, who takest away
the sins of the world,
spare us, O Lord.

Lamb of God, who takest away
the sins of the world,
Graciously hear us, O Lord,

Lamb of God, who takest away
the sins of the world,
Have mercy on us.

Pray for us, O holy Mother of God,
*That we may be made worthy of the
promises of Christ.*

Let us pray. — Grant, we beseech thee,
O Lord God, that we thy servants may enjoy
perpetual health of mind and body; and by
the intercession of the blessed Mary,
ever Virgin, may be delivered from
present sorrow, and obtain eternal joy. Through
Christ our Lord. — *Amen.*

Invite Mary to enter into your home and reign as a Queen: you will soon notice the difference in your Christian life.

Mary does what the best mother does in a home, indeed, more than what the best of mothers can do.

Mary brings a human smile and celestial happiness, even where sorrow had gained entrance.

Mary brings her heavenly light that shines serenely on souls, even where there was darkness or ignorance.

Mary softens hearts, makes things turn out well, sanctifies morals, induces the spread of benevolence among all.

Mary lends understanding and affection in husbands and wives, docility to children, patience, and the quality of industriousness to everyone.

Faith is revived through Mary, the hope of heaven is reinforced, charity is spread, and Christian life is established in the home.

A Story: Armand Godoy, the poet of the Litanies. — Born on the island of Cuba of Spanish immigrant parents, Armand Godoy wrote volumes in French which won him great renown.

He had made a rapid climb to fame when, weary of the affairs and the life of the world, he remembered that he had a soul — a poet's soul, in fact. Both the religious and artistic problems were happily resolved by him simultaneously; he humbly returned to God and joyously sang of his restored faith, thus imitating Copee, Huysmans, James and numberless other converts.

We particularly recall his "Ite Missa Est," a splendid poetic interpretation of the Holy Mass; also his "of the Canticle of Canticles at the Way of the Cross" and "The Litany of the Blessed Virgin."

Considering only this last book, "The Litany of the Blessed Virgin," we note that Godoy had the wonderful idea of explaining in poetry the titles we give to the Mother of God in the Litany of Loreto.

The literary value of this poem is varied: it cannot be assumed that his inspiration is lyrical to the same degree, but throughout there is a sincerity, a humility, a tenderness and an ardent enthusiasm for the theme that ranked Godoy high, indeed, among our religious poets.

"The Madonna," wrote Umberto Monti, in reference to Godoy, "is not only the Seat of Wisdom, but also Mother of good poetry, and our poets, if they draw near to her with reverence and devotion, will yet draw from David's harp new melodies to resound universally. The Madonna herself said that one day *all peoples would call her blessed.* We must not forget that there is room for all humanity in this blessedness of Mary, and who, if not a poet, should intone in the name of the Christian peoples a hymn of love and gratitude and praise to Our Lady?"

Prayer. — O sorrowful Virgin, all the trials, contradictions and infirmities which it shall please our Lord to send me I gladly offer to you in memory of your sorrows, so that every thought of my mind and every beat of my heart may be an act of compassion and love for you.

OTHER PRAYERS AND HYMNS

Immaculate Mary

Immaculate Mary,
Your praises we sing.
You reign now in splendor
With Jesus our King.
Ave, Ave, Ave Maria!
Ave, Ave Maria!

In heaven the blessed
Your glory proclaim
On earth we your children
Invoke your sweet name.
Ave, Ave, Ave Maria!
Ave, Ave Maria!

We pray for the Church,
Our true Mother on earth,
And beg you to watch
O'er the land of our birth.
Ave, Ave, Ave Maria!
Ave, Ave Maria!

O Most Holy One

O most holy one,
O most lowly one,
Loving virgin, Maria!
Mother, maid of fairest love,
Lady, Queen of all above,
Ora, ora pro nobis!

Virgin ever fair,
Mother, hear our prayer,
Look upon us, Maria!
Bring to us your treasure,
Grace beyond all measure;
Ora, ora pro nobis!

Sing of Mary

Sing of Mary, pure and lowly,
Virgin mother undefiled,
Sing of God's own son most holy,
Who became her little child.
Fairest child of fairest mother,
God the Lord who came to earth,
Word made flesh, our very brother,
Takes our nature by his birth.

Sing of Jesus, son of Mary,
In the home at Nazareth,
Toil and labor cannot weary,
Love enduring unto death.
Constant was the love he gave her,
Though he went forth from her side,
Forth to preach, and heal, and suffer,
Till on Calvary he died.

Joyful Mother, full of gladness,
In your arms, your Lord was borne,
Mournful Mother, full of sadness,
All your heart with pain was torn,

Glorious Mother, now rewarded,
With a crown at Jesus' hand,
Age to age your name recorded
Shall be blest in every land.

Glory be to God the Father;
Glory be to God the Son;
Glory be to God the Spirit;
Glory to the Three in One.
From the heart of blessed Mary,
From all saints the song ascends;
And the Church the strain re-echoes
Unto earth's remotest ends.

Ave Maris Stella

Star of ocean fairest,
Mother, God who bearest,
Virgin thou immortal,
Heaven's blissful portal.

Ave thou receivest;
Gabriel's word believest.
Change to peace and gladness
Eva's name of sadness.

Loose the bonds of terror,
Lighten bonded error;
All our ills repressing,
Pray for every blessing.

Mother's care displaying,
Offer Him thy praying
Who, when born our Brother
Chose thee for His Mother.

Virgin all excelling,
Gentle past our telling,
Pardoned sinners render
Gentle, chaste and tender.

In pure paths direct us,
On our way protect us,
Till on Jesus gazing,
We shall join thy praising.

Father, Son eternal,
Holy Ghost supernal,
With one praise we bless Thee,
Three in one confess Thee.

The Stabat Mater

At the cross her station keeping,
Stood the mournful Mother weeping,
Close to Jesus to the last.

Through her heart, His sorrow sharing,
All His bitter anguish bearing,
Now at length the sword had passed.

Oh, how sad and sore distressed
Was that Mother highly blest
Of the sole-begotten one!

Christ above in torment hangs;
She beneath beholds the pangs
Of her dying glorious Son.

Is there one who would not weep,
Whelmed in miseries so deep,
Christ's dear Mother to behold?

Can the human heart refrain
From partaking in her pain,
In that Mother's pain untold?

Bruised, derided, cursed, defiled,
She beheld her tender Child
All with bloody scourges rent.

For the sins of His own nation
She saw Him hang in desolation
Till His spirit forth He sent.

O my Mother, fount of love,
Touch my spirit from above;
Make my heart with yours accord.

Make me feel as you have felt,
Make my soul to glow and melt
With the love of Christ my Lord.

Holy Mother, pierce me through;
In my heart each wound renew
Of my Savior crucified.

Let me share with you His pain,
Who for all my sins was slain,
Who for me in torment died.

Let me mingle tears with you,
Mourning Him who mourned for me
All the days that I may live.

By the cross with you to stay,
There with you to weep and pray,
Is all I ask of you to give.

While my body here decays,
May my soul your goodness praise,
Safe in paradise with you. Amen.

Prayer Of Pope Pius XII

This prayer, dedicated to Mary Immaculate, was composed by the Pope for the Marian Year (December 8, 1953 — December 8, 1954), which was proclaimed to mark the centenary of the definition of the dogma of the Immaculate Conception.

Enraptured by the splendor of your heavenly beauty, and impelled by the anxieties of the world, we cast ourselves into your arms, O Immaculate Mother of Jesus and our Mother, Mary, confident of finding in your most loving heart appeasement of our ardent desires, and a safe harbor from the tempests which beset us on every side.

Though degraded by our faults and overwhelmed by infinite misery, we admire and praise the peerless richness of sublime gifts with which God has filled you, above every other mere creature, from the first moment of your conception until the day on which, after your assumption into heaven, He crowned you Queen of the Universe.

O crystal Fountain of faith, bathe our minds with the eternal truths! O fragrant Lily of all holiness, captivate our hearts with your heavenly perfume! O Conqueress of evil and death, inspire in us a deep horror of sin, which makes the soul detestable to God and a slave of hell!

O well-beloved of God, hear the ardent cry which rises up from every heart. Bend tenderly over our aching wounds. Convert the wicked, dry the tears of the afflicted and oppressed, comfort the poor and humble, quench hatreds, sweeten harshness, safeguard the flower of purity in youth, protect the holy Church, make all men feel the attraction of Christian goodness. In your name, resounding harmoniously in heaven, may they recognize that they are brothers, and that the nations are members of one family, upon which may there shine forth the sun of a universal and sincere peace.

Receive, O most sweet Mother, our humble supplications, and above all obtain for us that, one day, happy with you, we may repeat before your throne that hymn which today is sung on earth around your altars: You are all-beautiful, O Mary! You are the glory, you are the joy, you are the honor of our people! Amen.

A Prayer For Purity

Jesus, Mary and Joseph, I entrust and consecrate myself entirely to you — mind, heart and body. Guard and defend me always from every sin.

May my mind be uplifted to heavenly things; may my heart love God more and more; may I avoid every evil occasion. Hold me close to you, so that I may keep a watch on my internal and external senses and in heaven join the blessed company of the virgins. Amen.

Short Act of Consecration
To Jesus Through Mary

I am all Yours, and all that I possess I offer to You, my lovable Jesus, through Mary, Your most holy Mother.

For the Souls in Purgatory
(very dear to Mary's Heart)

Eternal rest grant unto them, O Lord, and let perpetual light shine upon them. May they rest in peace. Amen.

For the Dying

O St. Joseph, foster-father of Jesus Christ and true spouse of the Virgin Mary, pray for us and for the dying of this day (or of this night).

St. Bonaventure's
Marian Te Deum

We praise you, O Mother of God, we proclaim you Virgin and Mother!

The entire world venerates you as Spouse of the Eternal Father!

And to you all Angels, Archangels, Cherubim and Seraphim sing unceasingly:

Holy, Holy, Holy is the Mother of God, Mary ever Virgin!

Heaven and earth are filled with the majesty of your Son!

You are honored as Queen by the whole heavenly court!

You are invoked and praised as Mother of God by the entire world and by the holy Church.

You are Spouse and Mother of the eternal King, the temple and sanctuary of the Holy Spirit; the altar of the Blessed Trinity.

You are the Mediatrix between Jesus Christ and men, the Advocate of the poor!

You are, after Jesus, our only hope, Mistress of the world, Queen of Heaven!

We bow to you and salute you each day, O Mother of love!

Sweet and good Mary, in you we place all our hope, defend us for all eternity! Amen.

PART TWO — MARY, THE WORLD AND US

MARY ALWAYS AMONG US . . .

SHE BRINGS GOD'S MESSAGES TO US

Mary gave birth to Jesus, our Redeemer. As a devoted mother, she assisted him during the three years of his ministry. She was there when Jesus died on the cross, and when he was buried. She was there when Jesus ascended into heaven and she gathered the Apostles together in the Cenacle, and prayed with them until the Holy Spirit came and transformed them completely and made them ready to start the great work of evangelization.

Mary was the First Christian, the first member of the new Church. As Queen of the Apostles and Mother of the Church, she assisted and encouraged the Apostles in their work and gave example and encouragement to the first Christians.

After about sixty years of her physical life here on earth, Mary died and was assumed, body and soul, into heaven. But Mary never left us. Her memory and her spiritual assistance are with us forever.

Thousands of Churches, Shrines and Chapels were built and dedicated to her name. Millions of women were named after her. We all received from her a great number of graces . . . . She is spiritually here with us to help us to reach heaven, where she is, and where we want to be.

From time to time, down through the centuries, the Blessed Virgin has deigned to descend among her children in a visible manner. She always does so to communicate God's very important messages to us.

Mary's apparitions have been fairly numerous. Some of them have been recognized by the Church. Let us consider a few of these apparitions with their important messages.

Message from Guadalupe (1531). — On a summit of Tepeyac hill, a few miles north of Mexico City, in the midst of a resplendent light, the Blessed Virgin Mary appeared to Juan Diego, a recently converted Mexican Indian peasant, and said to him: *"My son, I love you tenderly, I praise your simple, sincere devotion, and your humility of heart pleases me. I want you to know that I am the Virgin Mother of God. It is my wish and the wish of God that a church be built on this place, wherein I shall reveal that I am a loving Mother to you and to souls who will confidently invoke my name. Listen, my son, to what I tell you now. Do not be troubled nor disturbed by anything; do not fear illness nor any distressing occurrence, nor pain. Am I not your mother? Am I not life and health? Have I not placed you on my lap and made you my responsibility? Do you need anything else?"*

The church was built as Our Lady requested, and was never closed to the people, notwithstanding persecutions, bombings and partial destruction.

In recent years, a new splendid and modern Basilica was inaugurated. Every year millions of people come on pilgrimage from everywhere. The place has become a center of prayers and worship; and many graces and blessings are received daily.

Our Lady of Guadalupe is now considered the heavenly Patroness of All the Americas.

Prayer to Our Lady of Guadalupe

Our Lady of Guadalupe, mystical rose, intercede for the Church, protect the Holy Father, help all who invoke you in their necessities. Since you are the ever Virgin Mary and Mother of the true God, obtain for us from your most holy Son the grace of a firm faith and a sure hope amid the bitterness of life, as well as an ardent love and the precious gift of final perseverance.

Message From La Salette (1846) — A little boy and a teenaged girl, Maximin Giraud and Melanie Mathieu, were tending cows in the little town of La Salette in southeastern France. One day, standing on a plateau, they beheld a luminous globe. The globe of light seemed to divide, and they saw a Lady seated on a large rock. She had her face in her hands, and she was weeping bitterly. The Lady slowly stood up, crossed her arms, and called the two children to her, telling them that she had some important news to communicate to them. She told the children that the hand of her Son was so strong and heavy that she could no longer hold it back, and that unless people did penance and obeyed God's law they would have much to suffer. Then, in a maternal, solicitous voice, the Lady admonished the two children to say their morning and night prayers well, and finally gave them God's message with these words: *"Well, my children, you will make this known to all my people."*

The two children did their best to convince the people to listen to Mary's Message. But the people persecuted them, laughed at them, and did not change their sinful way of living. So, the terrible calamities predicted took place.

The two children fearlessly continued to report accurately and without hesitation all that our Lady had said.

A spring close to the place where our Lady sat had burst forth and was freely flowing down the hill. Many miracles began to take place through the use of this miraculous water, and the people, visiting the place where our Lady appeared, started praying to her. A magnificent basilica was built on the site of the apparitions and became the center of prayers and miraculous happenings.

After many Church inquiries, and after hundreds of remarkable favors were obtained through the use of the miraculous water from the spring and recorded, Pope Pius IX approved the devotion to Our Lady of La Salette. He asked the children to convey in writing the secrets and to send them to him. He later exclaimed: *"These are the secrets of La Salette: Unless the world repent, it shall perish."*

The message of Our Lady of La Salette, given to the two children for the world in 1846, is still an important message today — to avoid sin and do penance, or terrible trials and sufferings will come upon the world.

Our Lady of La Salette
"Why do you weep, Oh Lady?"

"Why do you weep, oh Lady?
Why do you weep?"
"The hand of my Son grows heavy;
I fear it is too late,
I cannot hold it back any more
I must leave you to your fate."
Maximin and Melanie, in fear,
Stood before the Lady fair.
They heard the warning given,
The need for penance and prayer.
They told the country's people
What they had seen and heard
Some doubted, some believed,
Some took them at their word.
Many profited by that message
Given then for us.
It *still* holds true —
So, in Mary let us trust.
—*Sr. Mary Francis LeBlanc, O. Carm.*

INVOCATION

Our Lady of La Salette, reconciler of sinners, pray without ceasing for us who have recourse to thee.

Message from Lourdes (1858) — Bernadette Soubirous, a simple and innocent French girl, saw the figure of a marvelously beautiful Lady at the lonely grotto of Massabielle, Lourdes. The Lady was very kind and gracious, and she was dressed in a robe as white as snow, caught with a blue sash. Her hands were folded and she held a white Rosary with a gold chain. She was rapt in prayer. As Bernadette gazed upon that celestial vision, she could not comprehend its meaning. The radiant Lady then began to pass her fingers over the beads, indicating to Bernadette how dear the recitation of the Rosary was to her.

The message of God, communicated to us through the words of Our Lady, is: *"Please come here every day for a fortnight. Go and tell the priests to build a chapel on this spot. I want the people to come here in procession . . . . Pray — tell them to pray! Prayer and penitence. I AM THE IMMACULATE CONCEPTION. I do not promise to make you happy in this world, but in the next."*

Not one but several churches were built on the location. Thousands of pilgrims go to Lourdes every day, to pray and do penance for their sins and for the sins of the world.

Bernadette had been suffering much throughout her childhood from poverty and poor health. She was also thought to be stupid and ignorant, because her poor health caused her to miss a good deal of school. She was also misunderstood a great deal, especially since the apparitions began, and that caused her much heartbreak.

Bernadette became a nun and her sufferings continued even more severe than before. But in the last moments before she died, a smiling Mary was there to console her devoted child and take her soul to heaven.

Extraordinary cures are happening every day at Lourdes through the use of the water that sprung miraculously from the ground at the time of the apparitions, and many sinners are converted to God.

Prayer to Our Lady of Lourdes

O Immaculate Virgin Mary, you are the refuge of sinners, the health of the sick, and the comfort of the afflicted. By your appearances at the Grotto of Lourdes you made it a privileged sanctuary where your favors are given to people streaming to it from the whole world. Over the years countless sufferers have obtained the cure of their infirmities — whether of soul, mind, or body. Therefore I come with limitless confidence to implore your motherly intercessions. Loving Mother, obtain the grant of my requests. Let me strive to imitate your virtues on earth so that I may one day share your glory in heaven.

Message from Fatima (1917). — Three children of Fatima, Portugal — Lucia, Jacinta, and Francisco — while watching their sheep, suddenly saw the sun shining more brightly than usual, and a flash of lightning paralyzed them with terror. Then, looking to the right, they beheld a most beautiful and radiant Lady, more brilliant than the sun, standing on a small holm-oak tree. She wore a garment as white as snow, gathered at the neck by a golden cord; a white mantle embroidered in gold covered her whole person. From her joined hands fell a Rosary of pearl beads, at the end of which was a silver crucifix.

On October 13, 1917, 70,000 persons were at Cova da Iria when Our Lady appeared. Lucia asked her: "Who are you, and what do you want me to do?"

The vision answered: *"I am the Lady of the Rosary! I ask that a shrine be erected here in my honor. I have come to plead with all the faithful to amend their lives, to beg pardon for their sins, and to resolve never to offend the Lord again. Continue to say the Rosary devoutly every day. I promise that, if men will change their sinful life, I will answer their prayers, and the war [World War I] will end soon."*

In one of the apparitions, Our Lady told Lucia to insert between the mysteries of the Rosary the ejaculation: *"O my Jesus, forgive us our sins, save us from the fires of hell, lead all souls to heaven, especially those in most need of Your Mercy."*

Other important messages of Our Lady of Fatima are: "Pray, make the sacrifices for sinners. Many souls are lost because there is nobody to pray and make sacrifices for them." — *"The Lord wishes to spread the devotion to My Immaculate Heart."*

During the first apparition, Lucia courageously asked the Lady: "So, you said that you come from heaven! Am I going to heaven?"

"Yes," answered the Lady.
"And Jacinta?"
"She, too."
"And Francisco?"

The Virgin gazed upon the boy and said lovingly, *"He, too, but first he will have to say many Rosaries."*

Is it a coincidence, or a plan of God, that the Lourdes and Fatima messages "Prayer, avoiding sin, penance and consecration" coincide with the message of La Salette? Or, should we realize that God is talking to us and warning us through these messages, manifested to us through Our Lady?

Prayer to Our Lady of Fatima

O Most holy Virgin Mary, Queen of the most holy Rosary, you were pleased to appear to the children of Fatima and reveal a glorious message. We implore you, inspire in our hearts a fervent love for the recitation of the Rosary. By meditating on the mysteries of the redemption that are recalled therein may we obtain the graces and virtues that we ask, through the merits of Jesus, our Lord and Redeemer.

PICTURES AND STATUES:
The Sacred Heart of Jesus

"I will bless every place in which an image of my Heart is exposed and honored."

Those are the words of the Ninth Promise of the Sacred Heart of Jesus to St. Margaret Mary Alacoque.

Are Holy Pictures or Blessed Statues in the house things of the past, or things not contemplated in the interior design of a modern house?

Holy Pictures and Statues should appear in every Christian home!

A Crucifix, the symbol of our redemption, a sign of the greatest love shown to us by Jesus, the holy object which a dying person would like to kiss before death, should have a place of honor in every Christian home.

A statue or a picture of the Sacred Heart of Jesus, and a statue or a picture of the Immaculate Heart of Mary should also find a place in your house, as well as a picture or a statue of your favorite saint — such as, perhaps, St. Anthony.

All these holy objects will not disfigure the walls of your house; on the contrary, they will serve a purpose: to help you to live in the presence of God, keep evil away and bring blessings to your home.

As an example, a friend of mine kept many religious articles in her home, and one of them was a picture of the Sacred Heart. It held a place of honor in a corner of the living room for many years. Her Grandfather often sat and smoked in the chair directly under the picture. One day he fell asleep in the chair, and one of the lighted cigarettes dropped down in the chair, unnoticed. He got up and went out into the garage to work.

Slowly, the chair directly under the Sacred Heart picture caught fire. The flames were soaring high, licking the ceiling, destroying the chair and burning the side of the table next to it. Her Grandfather, who was alone on the property at the time, felt a sudden urge to go and check the house. He called the Fire Department, who speedily arrived before the flames could do any more damage. Of course, the chair under the Sacred Heart picture was totally demolished, but the picture itself was *completely untouched.* This is a very clear example of how the 9th Promise of the Sacred Heart proved itself.

When you are sad, discouraged, or depressed, take a prayerful look at one of these pictures, and you will soon realize that things could change within you in no time.

When you feel the need of strengthening your faith, a short prayer, privately said, before one of these holy images will surely and infallibly bring peace to your mind and love to your heart.

Your children, looking at these pictures, will ask you questions about Jesus and Mary, and join you in prayer.

A Holy Picture or a beautiful statue, as you have seen from the above example, cannot bring anything else into your house other than a *BLESSING.*

A little bottle of Holy Water kept in your house could come in very handy, especially when the Holy Eucharist is brought to a sick or an elderly person, or when the devil will disturb you with temptations: open the bottle, bless yourself with a sign of the cross, and the devil will immediately find out that your house is not the place for him to be.

A Story: The confidant of the Sacred Heart of Jesus, Saint Margaret Mary Alacoque. — The Sacred Heart of Jesus and the Immaculate Heart of Mary cannot be separated: they are one flame of love. I therefore thought it appropriate to summarize in this book a short history of the visions of St. Margaret Mary Alacoque and the beginning of the Devotion to the Sacred Heart of Jesus.

It took ten years for the Community of Paray-le-Monial to finally recognize that Sr. Margaret was favored by special visions from heaven. And it took a hundred years for the Church to even consider and seriously study these visions.

It was not until 1794 that Pope Pius VI gave full approbation to the Devotion of the Sacred Heart of Jesus. In 1856, Pope Pius IX approved and extended to the entire world a special Mass to the Sacred Heart of Jesus, and Pope Leo XIII, on April 2, 1898, recognized the Litany of the Sacred Heart of Jesus as a liturgical prayer.

The visions of Christ to St. Margaret Mary Alacoque occurred in the chapel at the convent of Paray-le-Monial, France, between 1673-75 — a little over three hundred years ago. Christ revealed Himself specifically as the God-man of the Heart! On the Feast of St. John in 1673, Christ revealed: "My Divine Heart is so passionately in love with men that it can no longer withhold the flames of that burning love; it must let them spread it abroad by means of you, and reveal itself to men to enrich them with its profound treasures which hold the graces they need to be saved from eternal loss." In 1674, Christ appeared and revealed his thoughts on the ingratitude of so many people. "I feel it more deeply than all that I suffered in My Passion. If they would only love Me in return, I would think little of all that I had done for them, and would wish, if I could, to do still more. But they meet my longings with coldness and contempt." It was on this occasion that the Master asked for Communions of reparation on the First Fridays of the month, and a Holy Hour on every Thursday evening from eleven to twelve, in reparation for people's sins. The "Great Revelation" came in June, 1675. "Behold this Heart," said Christ, "which has loved men that it has spared nothing even to exhausting and consuming itself in order to show them its love. And in return I receive from most men only ingratitude, by their irreverences and sacrileges, and by the coldness and contempt which they show Me in the Sacrament of Love. But what wounds Me even more deeply is that this is done by souls who are consecrated to Me." For these reasons, he asked for the Feast of the Sacred Heart and Communions of reparation on that day. "And I promise that my Heart will pour out abundantly the power of its love on those who pay it, or who cause others to pay it, honor."

In the course of His apparitions, Jesus promised many blessings to those who would open their hearts to His Heart. Sister Margaret recorded them throughout her letters, especially the "Great Promise" of dying in Christ's friendship and grace, if one made and lived the nine First Fridays of the month. It was only later that these promises were gathered into the listing familiar in later times.

The Twelve Promises of the Sacred Heart of Jesus

1. "I will give them all the graces necessary in their state of life.
2. "I will establish peace in their homes."
3. "I will comfort them in all their afflictions.
4. "I will be their secure refuge during life, and above all, in death.
5. "I will bestow abundant blessings upon all their undertakings.
6. "Sinners will find in My Heart the source and infinite ocean of mercy.
7. "Lukewarm souls shall become fervent.
8. "Fervent souls shall quickly mount to high perfection.
9. "I will bless every place in which an image of my Heart is exposed and honored.
10. "I will give to priests the gift of touching the most hardened hearts.
11. "Those who shall promote this devotion shall have their names written in my Heart.
12. "I promise you in the excessive mercy of My Heart that My all-powerful love will grant to all those who receive Holy Communion on the First Fridays in nine consecutive months the grace of final perseverance; they shall not die in My disgrace, nor without receiving their sacraments. My Divine Heart shall be their safe refuge in this last moment."

Short Family Prayer of Consecration

Lord Jesus Christ, we consecrate to you today ourselves and our family. The love for us and for all men that fills your Sacred Heart prompts us to pledge our lives in return.

We wish to live our lives in union with you. We wish to share your mission of bringing your Father's love to all humankind. We wish you to be the center of our hearts and of our home.

Lord Jesus Christ, accept this consecration of our family to you, and keep us ever one in your Most Sacred Heart. Amen.

Personal Prayer of Consecration

Reveal your Sacred Heart to me, O Jesus, and show me its attractions. Unite me to it forever. Grant that all my aspirations and all the beats of my heart, which never cease even while I sleep, may be a testimonial to you of my love for you, and may say to you: Yes, Lord, I am all yours. The pledge of my allegiance to you rests ever in my heart and will never cease to be there. Accept the slight amount of good that I do and be graciously pleased to repair all my wrong-doings, so that I may be able to bless you in time and eternity. AMEN.

Prayer of Reparation

My most loving Jesus, when I consider your tender Heart and see it full of mercy and tenderness towards sinners, my own heart is filled with joy and confidence that I shall be so kindly welcomed by you. Unfortunately, how many times have I sinned! But now, with Peter and with Magdalen, I weep for my sins and detest them because they offend you, infinite Goodness. Mercifully grant me pardon for them all; and let me die rather than offend you again, or at least let me live only to love you in return. AMEN.

THE LITANY OF THE SACRED HEART OF JESUS

Lord, have mercy on us. *Christ have mercy on us.*
Lord, have mercy on us. Christ, hear us. *Christ, graciously hear us.*

God, the Father of Heaven. *Have mercy on us...*
God, the Son, Redeemer of the world.
God, the Holy Spirit.
Holy Trinity, one God.
Heart of Jesus, Son of the Eternal Father.
Heart of Jesus, formed by the Holy Spirit in the womb of the Virgin Mother.
Heart of Jesus, substantially united to the Word of God.
Heart of Jesus, of Infinite Majesty.
Heart of Jesus, Sacred Temple of God.
Heart of Jesus, Tabernacle of the Most High.
Heart of Jesus, House of God and Gate of Heaven.
Heart of Jesus, burning furnace of charity.
Heart of Jesus, abode of justice and love.
Heart of Jesus, full of goodness and love.
Heart of Jesus, abyss of all virtues.
Heart of Jesus, most worthy of all praise.
Heart of Jesus, king and center of all hearts.
Heart of Jesus, in whom are all the treasures of wisdom and knowledge.

Heart of Jesus, in whom dwells the fullness of divinity.

Heart of Jesus, in whom the Father was well pleased.

Heart of Jesus, of whose fullness we have all received.

Heart of Jesus, desire of the everlasting hills.

Heart of Jesus, patient and most merciful.

Heart of Jesus, enriching all who invoke You.

Heart of Jesus, fountain of life and holiness.

Heart of Jesus, loaded down with opprobrium (disgrace).

Heart of Jesus, bruised for our offenses.

Heart of Jesus, obedient unto death.

Heart of Jesus, pierced with a lance.

Heart of Jesus, source of all consolation.

Heart of Jesus, our life and resurrection.

Heart of Jesus, our peace and reconciliation.

Heart of Jesus, victim for our sins.

Heart of Jesus, salvation of all who trust in You.

Heart of Jesus, hope of those who die in You.

Heart of Jesus, delight of all the Saints.

Lamb of God, who takes away the sins of the world.
Spare us, O Lord.

Lamb of God, who takes away the sins of the world.
Graciously hear us, O Lord.

Lamb of God, who takes away the sins of the world.
Have mercy on us.
Verse: Jesus, meek and humble of heart.
Response: Make our hearts like to yours.

Let us pray. Almighty and eternal God, look upon the Heart of your most beloved Son, and upon the praise and satisfaction which he offers You in the name of sinners; and to those who implore Your mercy, in Your great goodness, grant forgiveness in the name of the same Jesus Christ, Your Son, who lives and reigns with You forever and ever. AMEN.

MEDALS:

The Miraculous Medal

Not many years ago, the Perpetual Novena of Our Lady of the Miraculous Medal was widely practiced on one of the weekdays. Many people faithfully attended this devotion every week. The Rosary was recited, hymns in honor of Our Blessed Mother were sung by the entire community, a short sermon was preached, Medals and Religious Articles were blessed, and everything was concluded with the Solemn Benediction of the Most Blessed Sacrament.

People were used to acquire, have blessed and wear the specially coined Medal called the Miraculous Medal.

Many blessings and even miraculous happenings came to the people of God through this devotion.

For our spiritual good, we sincerely hope and desire that this devotion will be revitalized and practiced again.

The Miraculous Medal was revealed by the Blessed Virgin Mary in a vision granted St. Catherine Laboure, a Daughter of Charity of St. Vincent de Paul, at the Paris Motherhouse, Nov. 27, 1830. The Virgin stood upon a globe, crushing a serpent beneath her foot. Rays of light, symbolizing graces, streamed from her outstretched hands. Written around her was the prayer: "O Mary, conceived without sin, pray for us who have recourse to thee." The vision reversed revealing an "M" surmounted by a bar and cross. Beneath were the Hearts of Jesus and Mary, the one crowned with thorns, the other pierced with a sword. Twelve stars encircled the whole. A voice spoke: *"Have a medal struck after this model. All who wear it will receive great graces. They should wear it around the neck."*

The first medals were struck, with permission of Archbishop de Quelen of Paris, June 30, 1832. So many remarkable favors followed that people called the medal "miraculous." A canonical inquiry at Paris (1836) certified its supernatural origin and efficacy. Papal approval followed the instantaneous conversion of Alphonse Ratisbone, a Jew hostile to Catholicism, to whom the Madonna of the Medal appeared in the church of San Andrea delle Fratte, Rome, January 20, 1842.

Pius IX (June 20, 1847) approved the Association of the Children of Mary, requested of St. Catherine by the Virgin, granting it all indulgences enjoyed by the *Prima Primaria* (1584); the medal is its badge. Leo XIII (July 23, 1894) honored the medal with a Mass and Office for November 27, proper to the Congregation of the Missions (Vincentian Fathers) and Daughters of Charity. Pius X (June 3, 1905) established the Association of the Miraculous Medal, granting it the indulgences and privileges enjoyed by the Confraternity of the Blue Scapular; all invested in the medal are members. Blessing of, and investiture in, the medal is proper to the Congregation of the Mission.

Rev. Joseph A. Skelly inaugurated the Miraculous Medal Perpetual Novena at Mary's Central Shrine, in Philadelphia, December 8, 1930. The Devotion, indulgenced by Pius XI, Pius XII, John XXIII, and

Paul VI, has spread to 4,500 churches throughout America and the world.

An Act of Consecration to
Our Lady of the Miraculous Medal

O Virgin Mother of God, Mary Immaculate, we dedicate and consecrate ourselves to you under the title of Our Lady of the Miraculous Medal. May this Medal be for each one of us a sure sign of your affection for us and a constant reminder of our duties towards you. Even while wearing it, may we be blessed by your loving protection and preserved in the grace of your Son. O most powerful Virgin, Mother of our Savior, keep us close to you every moment of our lives. Obtain for us, your children, the grace of a happy death; so that, in union with you, we may enjoy the bliss of heaven forever. Amen.

V. O Mary, conceived without sin,
R. Pray for us who have recourse to you.
(3 times)

Let us pray. O Lord Jesus Christ, who have vouchsafed to glorify by numberless miracles the Blessed Virgin Mary, immaculate from the first moment of her conception, grant that all who devoutly implore her protection on earth, may eternally enjoy Your presence in heaven, who, with the Father and the Holy Spirit, live and reign, God, for ever and ever. Amen.

SCAPULARS:
The Brown Scapular
and the Green Scapular

The Brown Scapular. — The place that attracted me most on my pilgrimage to the Holy Land in 1986 was the last place I visited: Mount Carmel, not far away from Nazareth. I was there only two hours, but a strange force was pushing me to return to the altar of Our Lady of Mt. Carmel. I did that at least ten times, kneeling there and praying while looking at the beautiful statue of Our Lady.

850 years before the birth of Christ, Elijah the Prophet and his companions lived on top of Mt. Carmel. They were the first to honor Mary, the future Mother of the Messiah. Centuries after, the Crusaders found a number of holy men living in caves, calling themselves *The Hermits of Our Lady of Mt. Carmel.* They were the precursors of the Carmelite Order.

In 1245, a holy man, Simon Stock (who later was proclaimed a saint), was elected Superior General of the Carmelite Order in the West. Discouraged by the many difficulties the Order was encountering, he redoubled his prayers and pleadings to Our Lady asking for help and a sign. During the early morning of July 16, 1251, Simon's cell was flooded with a great light. Our Lady, accompanied by a multitude of angels, appeared to Simon, holding the scapular of the Order in her hands. She said to him, *"Receive, my beloved son, this Scapular of your Order. This shall be to you and to all Carmelites a privilege that whosoever dies clothed in this shall never suffer eternal* fire. It is the badge of salvation, a protection in danger, a pledge of peace and eternal alliance.''

The devil continued to stir up opposition, but the Carmelites, undaunted, continued to work for their Queen and Mother. Our Lady of Mt. Carmel appeared to Pope John XXII urging him to take the Order under his special protection, and made a second promise to all those who wore the Scapular. Mary promised that she would assist the souls of the members in purgatory and deliver them from their sufferings on the first Saturday after their death.

The second traditional promise of Our Blessed Mother in favor of those who wear her Brown Scapular of Mt. Carmel is called "The Sabbatine Privilege," and was made known to us through a Papal Bull issued March 3, 1322, by Pope John XXII, *"On Saturday, as many as I shall find in Purgatory I shall free."*

To Our Lady Of The Scapular

O most blessed and immaculate Virgin, ornament and splendor of Carmel, you who look with an eye of special kindness on those who wear the Blessed Habit, look down benignly upon me and cover me with the mantle of your special protection. Strengthen my weakness with your power; enlighten the darkness of my mind with your wisdom; increase in me faith, hope and love. Adorn my soul with such graces and virtues as will ever be pleasing to your divine Son and to you. Assist me in life, and console me in death, with your most holy presence,

and present me to the most Holy Trinity as your devoted servant and child; that I may eternally bless and praise you in paradise. Amen.

The Green Scapular. — Also called the Scapular of the Immaculate Heart of Mary this is another gift of our Blessed Mother to all of us.

Sr. Justine Bisqueyburu, of the Daughters of Charity, on January 28, 1840, was favored with a celestial vision. Our Lady appeared to her clothed in a long white robe over which hung a bright blue mantle. Her hair, which fell loosely over her shoulders, was not covered with a veil, and in her hands she held her heart, from the top of which issued brilliant rays. To the dignity of her bearing was joined the dazzling brightness of celestial beauty.

The same apparition was repeated four or five times during the principal feasts of the Blessed Virgin.

Sister Bisqueyburu, on September 8, 1840, feast of the Nativity of the Blessed Virgin, was favored during prayer with an apparition of the Mother of God, who held in her right hand her heart surrounded by flames, and in her left a sort of scapular, consisting of a single piece of green cloth suspended from a cord of the same color. On one side was a picture of the Blessed Virgin as she had shown herself in the apparitions; on the other, a heart all inflamed with rays more brilliant than the sun, and clearer than crystal.

This heart pierced with a sword was surrounded by an oval inscription, surmounted by a cross. The inscription read: *"Immaculate Heart of Mary, pray for us now and at the hour of our death."* At the same time an interior voice revealed to the Sister the meaning of this vision. She understood that this new scapular would contribute to the conversion of those who have no faith, and above all, procure for them a happy death, and that it should be distributed immediately with confidence.

The manner of using the scapular was indicated by the Blessed Virgin. Since it is not the badge of a confraternity but simply a double image attached to a single piece of cloth and suspended from a cord, the formalities of a scapular are not required for the benediction and imposition. It suffices that it be blessed by a priest. It may be placed in the clothing, on the bed, or simply in the room. The only prayer to be recited daily is *"Immaculate Heart of Mary, pray for us now and at the hour of our death."*

The Green Scapular was twice approved by Pope Pius IX, in 1863 and again in 1870.

Prayer To The Immaculate Heart of Mary

Mary, Virgin most powerful and Mother of mercy, Queen of heaven and Refuge of sinners, we consecrate ourselves to your Immaculate Heart. We consecrate to you our very being and our whole life; all that we have, all that we love, all that we are. To you we give our bodies, our hearts, and our souls; to you we give our homes, our families, our country. We desire that all

that is in us and around us may belong
to you, and may share in the benefits
of your motherly blessing.

That this act of consecration may be truly
fruitful and lasting, we renew this day
at your feet the promises of our baptism
and our first Holy Communion.

We pledge ourselves to profess courageously and at all times the truths of our
holy Faith, and to live as befits Catholics
who are submissive to all the directions of
the Pope, and the Bishops in communion
with him. We pledge ourselves to keep
the commandments of God and His Church,
in particular to keep holy the Lord's Day.
We likewise pledge ourselves to make con-
soling practices of the Christian religion,
and, above all, Holy Communion, an important part of our lives, in so far as we
shall be able to do so.

Finally, we promise you, O glorious
Mother of God and loving Mother of men,
to devote ourselves wholeheartedly to
the spreading of devotion to your Immaculate Heart, in order to hasten and assure, through the queenly rule of your Immaculate Heart, the coming of the kingdom
of the Sacred Heart of your Son, in our own
hearts and in those of all men, in our
country and in all the world, as in heaven
so on earth. Amen.

DEVOTION OF THE FIVE CONSECUTIVE FIRST SATURDAYS

It is my firm opinion that the Devotion of the Five First Saturdays will be one of the most important devotions in honor of Our Blessed Mother.

Little known and practiced now, it will eventually become very popular among the People of God.

The reasons? Mary personally requested that this Devotion be introduced in the Church, and secondly, it is strictly and intimately connected with all the extraordinary events that happened at Fatima in 1917.

On December 10, 1925 the Blessed Virgin appeared to Sister Marie of the Sorrows in her room, and revealed her Immaculate Heart. Our Lady asked Sr. Marie to reveal this message to the world: *"I promise to assist at the hour of death with the graces necessary for salvation, all those who on the First Saturday of five consecutive months, shall confess, receive Holy Communion, recite five decades of my Rosary, and keep me company for a quarter of an hour while meditating on the mysteries of the Rosary, with the intention of offering me reparation."*

This Devotion could be practiced, individually, in any place, or in the church as a group, as a Communitarian public prayer.

Rules and method you can follow:

1) Be sure it is done on Five First Consecutive Saturdays.

2) Make a good confession (if necessary) and receive Holy Communion each Saturday.

3) Recite five decades of the Rosary, adding at the end of each decade this prayer taught to the children

on July 13, 1917, by Our Lady herself, "O my Jesus, forgive us our sins, deliver us from the fires of hell, draw the souls of all to heaven, especially those in greatest need."

4) Keep Mary's company for fifteen minutes while meditating on the fifteen mysteries of the Rosary.

5) Practice this Devotion with the intention of doing reparation for sins as Mary requested.

6) Conclusion: recite the following Prayers:

Immaculate Heart of Mary, full of love of God and men, I consecrate myself entirely to you. I entrust to you the salvation of my soul. With your help may I hate sin, love God and my neighbor, and reach eternal life together with those whom I love.

Mediatrix of Grace and Mother of Mercy, your Divine Son has merited boundless treasures of grace by His sufferings, which He has confided to you for us, your children. Filled with confidence in your Motherly Heart, I come to you with my pressing needs. For the sake of the Sacred Heart of Jesus, obtain for me the favor I ask.

(Mention your request).

Dearest Mother, if what I ask for should not be according to God's will, pray that I may receive that which will be of greater benefit to my soul. May I experience the

kindness of your Motherly Heart and the power of your intercession with Jesus during life and at the hour of my death.

V. Immaculate Heart of Mary,
R. Pray for us, who have recourse to you.

Let us pray: O God of infinite goodness and mercy, fill our hearts with a great confidence in our Most Holy Mother, whom we invoke under the title of the Immaculate Heart of Mary, and grant us by Her most powerful intercession all the graces, spiritual and temporal, which we need. Through Christ our Lord. Amen.

MARY SEEN BY POPE JOHN PAUL II

Mary As Model of Faith

"And Blessed is she who believed that there would be a fulfillment of what was spoken to her from the Lord" (Lk 1:45).

The Solemnity of Pentecost 1987 inaugurated the Marian Year. The Marian Year is an invitation and an exhortation, addressed to the whole Church, to every community and every Christian, to draw near to the Mother of Christ precisely in a pilgrimage of faith, to renew, near the end of the second millennium, a faith which, in the heart and life of Mary, has become the Church's journey throughout centuries and millennia.

God's love

On her visit to Elizabeth, the Virgin of Nazareth responds to her cousin's greeting with the words of the *Magnificat:* "He who is mighty has done great things for me, and holy is his name" (Lk 1:49).

Mary's faith is expressed in these words — indeed, it is expressed in the whole of the *Magnificat* but in these words in a special way. Therefore we should note and meditate upon these words in a special mystery of the Mother of God, if we are to follow Mary on her journey of faith.

Faith is the awareness of "the great things done by the Almighty." These "great things," whether in the order of creation, or still more in the order of redemption, speak of him as the primary source of the gift. That source is called Love: "God is love" (1 John 4:8).

Precisely as love, and for love, "he made himself poor so that we might become rich" (2 Cor 8:9). The Virgin of Nazareth has a profound awareness of this truth and expresses it in the *Magnificat*. She herself is the first among these "poor," to whom the living God has freely become as close as possible.

Struggles against evil

The liturgy of the Solemnity of the Assumption of the Blessed Virgin Mary shows us, in the words of the Book of Revelation, a woman who fights against the dragon. In this way, the final book of Scripture refers to the first, to the Book of Genesis. Mary, who has believed absolutely in God-Love, is found, in the course of human and Church history, in a certain sense at the center of this struggle against evil, a struggle which the prince of darkness, "that ancient serpent" (Rev 12:9) wages against God and the whole Divine order of love, grace, gift and holiness.

To share in the faith of the blessed Virgin means to share also in this struggle: within oneself, in the context of one's own life and daily responsibilities.

In this combat Mary is victorious through faith. "This is our victory: our faith," as St. John has written.

"He who is mighty has done great things for me." These words, spoken at the Visitation, receive final confirmation in the mystery of Mary's Assumption into heaven. "For behold, henceforth all generations will call me blessed" (Lk 1:48).

Model of faith, virtue

The Council expresses it as follows: "Finally the Immaculate Virgin, preserved free from all stain of original sin, was taken up body and soul into heavenly glory when her earthly life was over, and exalted by the Lord as Queen over all things, that she might be more fully conformed to her Son, the Lord of lords (cf. Rev 19:16) and conqueror of sin and death" (*Lumen Gentium, 59*).

"But while in the Most Blessed Virgin the Church has already reached that perfection . . . , the faithful still strive to conquer sin and increase in holiness. And so they turn their eyes to Mary who shines forth to the whole community of the elect as the model of virtues" (*LG* 65).

Mary, model of virtue, above all, model of faith. As we contemplate her, let us ask her to go before us on our path of faith, to direct us, to support us. Let us raise our eyes to her and ask her to obtain for us always the gift of faith, the power of faith, the joy of faith: to make us "conquer sin and increase in holiness."

TEACH US THE PATHS OF FAITH

Mother of the Church, teach the People of God the paths of faith, hope, and charity!

Help us to live in the truth of the consecration of Christ for the entire human family of the contemporary world.

Entrusting to you, O Mother, the world, all individuals, and all peoples, we also entrust to you the "consecration of the world," placing it in your Motherly Heart!

O Immaculate Heart, help us to overcome the threat of evil, which so easily takes root in the hearts of people today and which in its immeasurable effects weighs heavily upon the present life and seems to close the paths to the future!

REDEMPTORIS MATER

Excerpt from the Conclusion of the Encyclical letter of Pope John Paul II "Mother of the Redeemer"

At the end of the daily Liturgy of the Hours, among the invocations addressed to Mary by the Church is the following:

"Loving mother of the Redeemer, gate of heaven, star of the sea, assist your people who have fallen yet strive to rise again. To the wonderment of nature you bore your Creator!"

"To the wonderment of nature!" These words of the antiphon express that wonderment of faith which accompanies the mystery of Mary's divine motherhood. In a sense, it does so in the heart of the whole of creation, and, directly, in the heart of the whole People of God, in the heart of the Church. How wonderfully far God has gone, the Creator and Lord of all things, in the "revelation of himself" to man! How clearly he has bridged all the spaces of that infinite "distance" which separates the Creator from the creature! If in himself he remains ineffable and unsearchable, still more ineffable and unsearchable is he in the reality of the Incarnation of the Word, who became man through the Virgin of Nazareth.

If he has eternally willed to call man to share in the divine nature (2 Pt 1:4), it can be said that he has matched the "divinization" of man to humanity's historical conditions, so that even after sin he is ready to restore at a great price the eternal plan of his love through the "humanization" of his Son, who is of the same being as himself. The whole of creation, and more directly man himself, cannot fail to be amazed at this gift in which he has become a sharer, in the Holy Spirit: "God so loved the world that he gave his only Son" (Jn 3:16).

THE LIGHT OF HOPE

Heed, O Mother of Christ, this cry "charged with the suffering" of all human beings! "Charged with the suffering" of entire societies!

Help us by the power of the Holy Spirit to overcome every sin: the sin of the individuals and the "sin of the world," sin in every one of its manifestations.

Let there be revealed once more, in the history of the world, the infinite salvific power of the Redemption: the power "of merciful Love!"

May it arrest evil and transform consciences!

In your Immaculate Heart let the light of Hope be manifested to all human beings!

Liturgical Feasts of the Blessed Virgin Mary

There are sixteen feasts throughout the liturgical year, established by the Church, to honor Our Blessed Mother and to rekindle our love towards her.

Celebrate each feast with joy and devotion, by meditating on the title of the feast, saying some extra prayers to Mary, and especially by going to church on that day.

Each Marian feast, celebrated with faith, will bring us many new graces and special blessings from heaven:

January 1 — Solemnity of Mary, the Mother of God
February 2 — Presentation of Jesus in the Temple
February 11 — Our Lady of Lourdes
March 25 — The Annunciation
May 31 — The Visitation/Immaculate Heart of Mary
July 16 — Our Lady of Mt. Carmel
August 5 — Dedication of St. Mary Major
August 15 — Assumption of the Blessed Virgin Mary
August 22 — The Queenship of Mary
September 8 — The Birth of Mary
September 15 — Our Lady of Sorrows
October 7 — Our Lady of the Rosary
November 21 — The Presentation of Mary
December 8 — The Immaculate Conception
December 12 — Our Lady of Guadalupe
December 25 — Christmas, The Birth of Our Lord

" Just as there was never a love like hers, so also there was never a sorrow like hers." — *Richard of St. Victor*

"From the moment of Jesus' birth, the black shadow of the cross weighed heavily on Mary's heart." — *Bossuet*

"She knew that she was raising the most lovable of sons for the most horrible of torments possible to man." — *St. Cyriacus*

"Whoever wishes the grace of the divine Spirit must seek the Flower on this stem; by the stem he will reach the Flower, and by the Flower, the Spirit." — *St. Bonaventure*

"Through you, O Mary, we have access to the Son, so that He who was given to us through your love will receive us through your love." — *St. Bernard*

"With divine grace the apostolate of suffering is possible to everyone. And since everyone has something to suffer, we can change into virtue this inevitable suffering." — *James Alberione*

A Story: St. Alphonsus Rodriguez. — One of Mary's great devotees was St. Alphonsus Rodriguez.

On July 25, 1531, Alphonsus was born in Segovia, an industrial and commercial city of old Castile. As a child he showed his devotion to Mary, a devotion which ever increased with the passing of the years. After a somewhat turbulent life, he recognized, in his trials, God's voice calling him to the Jesuits, and he answered promptly. He repented of his past life and armed himself with the powerful weapons of penance and prayer. And Mary showed him, even in a tangible way, how much this pleased her.

When his two years as a novice were completed in a most exemplary manner, Alphonsus was permitted to take his vows in religion. He made it a practice to honor the Blessed Virgin by the daily recitation of the Rosary, of the Office of the Immaculate, of the Litany, of twelve Hail Holy Queens, and twelve Hail Marys, with the intention of sanctifying the hours of the day and night.

The Hail Mary became as his breath, his most spontaneous ejaculation. He had also made a pact with his Guardian Angel to the effect that while he slept, the Angel would recite the Hail Mary, so that the salutation to his Queen would not cease.

Alphonsus made a special effort to celebrate, with great devotion and fervor, all the Feasts in honor of the Blessed Virgin Mary, scattered all through the liturgical year.

He progressed daily in the virtues of prayer and of mortification. These virtues led him to the highest and continuous union with God so that, at times, just by saying, "Lord," or "My Beloved is with me and I am with Him," he would be consumed with ecstasy.

However, that which made of Alphonsus a hero and martyr were the great temptations with which the Lord tried him, and which he, as a valiant soldier, successfully overcame.

Alphonsus' *zeal* for the salvation of souls was immense. He prayed incessantly for the missionaries and preachers of his Society.

His writings, full of great love of God, were also the instruments of his zeal.

After a life expended for the Lord and after an ecstasy of three consecutive days, Alphonsus flew to his "Loves" as he habitually called Jesus and Mary, pronouncing their adorable Names for the last time. On January 15, 1888, Pope Leo XIII numbered him among the saints.

Prayer. — O Virgin most pure, by your motherly heart so full of anguish at the loss of your dear Jesus, obtain for me the virtue of chastity and the gift of knowledge.

A VERY SPECIAL PRAYER TO THE BLESSED VIRGIN,
Mother of God and Our Mother

O most beautiful Flower of Mount Carmel, Fruitful Vine, Splendor of Heaven, blessed Mother of the Son of God, Immaculate Virgin, assist me in this my necessity. O Star of the sea, help me, and show me herein you are my Mother.

O Holy Mary, Mother of God, Queen of Heaven and Earth, I humbly beseech you from the bottom of my heart, to succor me in this necessity: there are none that can withstand your power.

O show me herein you are my Mother. O Mary, conceived without sin, pray for us who have recourse to thee. *(3 times).*

Sweet Mother, I place this cause in your hands. *(3 times).*

EVERY SATURDAY IS "MARY'S DAY"

Saturday is a very special day for me. When I awaken in the morning, the first thought and the first image that comes to my mind is that of the Blessed Virgin Mary.

Every Saturday of the year is dedicated to Mary. It is "Mary's Day."

Even the Liturgy of the Church favors Mary on that day. If Saturday is an open day (a day without the commemoration of a Saint), the Church recommends to honor Mary with a special Mass, called "St. Mary on the Sabbath," and the priests can say the Office of the Blessed Virgin Mary.

Every Saturday welcome Mary with the Devotion of the "Three Hail Marys"; go to Mass if you can; do something special to please her: an act of kindness, a short prayer when passing in front pf Mary's picture, the recitation of the "Angelus."

Every devotee of Mary performs everything under her gaze. Brief remembrances, tiny aspirations sent in flight, fleeting glances at her images are testimonials of love that he gives her continually. Alone or in the company of others, along the street or in his room, he is always murmuring some ejaculation to her. In doubts and struggles, in pains and joys, the Hail Mary passes from his lips to the heart of the Virgin and flows back to him in waves of graces.

St. John Eudes wrote: "Live in Mary's heart, love what she loves, desire what she desires, and you will have peace, joy, and sanctity."

O Mary, it is sweet to turn my first look upon you in the morning, to walk beneath your

mantle during the day, to fall asleep under your gaze at night!

Give me a penitent life so that I may have a holy death and may one day raise my voice with those of the saints, to praise you in paradise!

A Story: Blessed Contardo Ferrini. — Contardo Ferrini was born of devout parents in 1859. He received a fine Christian upbringing to which he corresponded fully. After successfully completing his classical studies, he went to the University of Pavia where, because of his precocious mind, he acquired a high degree of learning in a brief span of time.

In this young man's room, an image of Mary, Seat of Wisdom, occupied a place of honor. To her, he had entrusted his future. At the age of twenty-two, he received his degree in law, and at twenty-four, with a rich and profound cultural background, he embarked upon his career as Professor of History of Roman Law. He spoke Latin, Greek, Hebrew, German, French, English, Syrian and Spanish fluently.

He soon began to publish important works, and he diligently responded to the vocation he received from God by breaking and distributing the bread of truth among the ignorant. He led a retiring, humble, charitable, and virtuous life, always practicing the evangelical counsels.

Contardo Ferrini wrote pages of great beauty on various feasts of Mary. Regarding the feast of the Annunciation he comments as follows on the words, *Behold the handmaid of the Lord; be it done unto me according* to Thy word: "Never before was such true and wondrous humility expressed; never before was any creature raised to such stupendous honors by God and who was at the same time so convinced of her nothingness. It has been well said that Mary pleased God because of her virginity but conceived Our Savior because of her great humility."

Regarding the feast of Mary's Visitation, Ferrini said "Elizabeth greets her . . . . And Mary feels very lowly as she considers God's tenderness for she realizes that He wills to choose little ones for great deeds and that His goodness is greatest toward the weak. Then she bursts into that hymn which we should intone with the Angels after Communion : 'My soul magnifies the Lord.' He is to be admired who can find cause for humility even from praise."

Because of his great love for her, Contardo remained faithful to Mary until his death at age forty-three.

Prayer. — O Mary Immaculate, the precious name of Mother of Good Hope, with which we honor you, fills our hearts to overflowing with the sweetest consolation and moves us to hope for every blessing from you.

Mother of God, Remember Me

Mother of God, remember me
To the Heart of Christ Thy Son;
Remember me, Mother, through all my years
Till my work on earth is done.
Mother of God, remember me

When I reach the vast unknown;
Remember me, Mother, and plead my cause
When I stand to be judged alone.
Mother of God, remember me
As I pass my final goal;
Lily white village maid, Mother of God,
Tell Jesus you love my soul.
Mother of God, remember me
in the Court of thy Son Divine
Let me praise and love Him
forever more,
near that beautiful Heart of Thine.

Alma de la Cruz

THE SEVEN WORDS OF THE BLESSED VIRGIN

With the exception of the Magnificat, Mary's words were few and brief but most meaningful. The Gospel records seven phrases uttered by Mary.

The first was one of virginal reserve: *"How shall this happen, since I do not know man?"* (Luke 1:34).

The second was one of faithful obedience: *"Behold the handmaid of the Lord; be it done to me according to thy word"* (Luke 1:38).

The third was one of reverent modesty: she *"saluted Elizabeth"* (Luke 1:40).

The fourth was one of grateful joy: *My soul magnifies the Lord"* (Luke 1:46).

The fifth was one of authoritative gentleness: *"Son, why hast Thou done so to us?"* (Luke 2:48).

The sixth was one of tender charity: *"They have no wine"* (John 2:3).

The seventh was one of firm faith: *"Do whatever He tells you"* (John 2:5).

A Story: St. Ephrem loved and praised Mary. — The life of St. Ephrem is the life of a great ascetic and mystic, as well as of a most active Apologist and adversary of all heresies.

He was born of pagan parents in Mesopotamia in 306, during the reign of Constantine the Great, when Christianity was spreading rapidly everywhere. As soon as Ephrem came to know the Christian Faith, he embraced it enthusiastically. When his father grew aware of his conversion, he turned him out of the house. Bearing love of religion as his only possession, Ephrem then went to the Bishop of his city. Here he revealed the rarity of his talents to such an extent that although he was only twenty-five, he was assigned a teaching position and ordained a deacon. Later, Ephrem retired to Edessa where he spent the rest of his life. It was there that he wrote the greater part of his works, which have come down to us. He lived as an anchorite on a mountain where it was possible for many disciples to gather about him.

Ephrem was a master in writing hymns and using them to fight the heretics of his time. He would take the popular songs of the heretical groups and, using their melodies, compose beautiful hymns embodying orthodox doctrine. Ephrem became one of the first to introduce song into the Church's public worship as a means of instruction for the faithful. Singing is an excellent way of expressing and creating a community spirit of unity, as well as joy. Ephrem's hymns lent luster to the Christian assemblies.

St. Ephrem's devotion to the Blessed Virgin Mary was something out of the ordinary, as his numerous writings on the Blessed Virgin attest. These works could only have been the fruit of a sublime mind occupied wholly with the thought of Mary and of the tenderest of hearts which, not content to have tested the ineffable sweetness of such a love, desired to share it with others.

The fundamental thought of St. Ephrem's Marian doctrine is that Mary's sublime prerogatives, described by him so amply and richly, are a natural consequence of the privilege reserved to her of being the Mother of Jesus. Having established this principle, Ephrem proceeds to affirm, with a logical claim of reasoning, that Mary Most Holy was conceived without sin. He sets forth the truth with admirable clarity and says, "Mary was immaculate and free of even the least sin."

St. Ephrem's motive in all his writings on the Virgin is to imbue us with a great trust in Mary, and to make us love her with a love similar to the love borne her by the Celestial Father, Whose daughter she is, by Jesus Christ, Whose Mother she is, by the Holy Spirit, Whose mystical Spouse she is.

And let us, who know our great need for Mary, repeat often with St. Ephrem during the course of our trial on earth, "O Immaculate Virgin, protect us and guard us beneath the wings of your tender pity."

St. Ephrem died at Edessa around the year 373.

Two Beautiful Prayers of St. Ephrem, the Syrian:

Prayer of Praise

O pure and Immaculate blessed Virgin, the sinless Mother of your Son, the mighty Lord of the universe, you who are all pure and all holy, the hope of the hopeless and sinful, we sing your praises. We bless you, as full of every grace, you who bore the God-Man: we all bow low before you; we invoke you and implore your aid. Rescue us, O holy and pure Virgin, from every necessity that presses upon us and from all the temptations of the devil. Be our intercessor and advocate at the hour of death and judgment; deliver us from the fire that is not extinguished and from the outer

darkness; make us worthy of the glory of your Son, O dearest and most clement Virgin Mother. You indeed are our only hope, most sure and sacred in God's sight, to whom be honor and glory, majesty and dominion for ever and ever, world without end. Amen.

To The Immaculate Queen

O Virgin most pure, wholly unspotted, O Mary, Mother of God, Queen of the universe, you are above all the saints, the hope of the elect and the joy of all the blessed. It is you who has reconciled us with God; you are the only refuge of sinners and the safe harbor of those who are shipwrecked; you are the consolation of the world, the ransom of captives, the health of the weak, the joy of the afflicted, and the salvation of all. We have recourse to you, and we beseech you to have pity on us. Amen.

The Immaculate Heart of Mary
. . . and Russia

So much is said about the apparitions of Fatima, the conversations between Our Lady and the three children, the invitation about doing penance for the many sins of the world, which are sending so many sinners to hell, the encouragement to say the Rosary, often and devoutly, but not much is said about the desires of Our Blessed Lady and her plans for peace in the world and the conversion of Russia.

To me, what Mary wishes and wants is as important, if not more, as all the above things put together!

Mary said, *"The Lord wishes to spread the devotion to my Immaculate Heart . . . . If my requests are granted, Russia will be converted . . . there will be peace . . . . If my requests are not granted, Russia will spread her errors throughout the world, causing new wars and persecutions to the Church . . ."*

Our Lady of Fatima also promised, *"But in the end, if this devotion is practiced, my Immaculate Heart will triumph . . . Russia will be converted . . . there will be peace in the world and salvation for all sinners."*

Why a specific devotion to the Immaculate Heart of Mary?

Immorality of every kind is flooding the entire world today. Only by looking at the loving and Immaculate Heart of Mary, imitating her undefiled and pure Heart, and praying to her, can this very destructive, immoral flood be stopped.

Mary, according to Sr. Marie of the Sorrows, (Lucia), asked *specifically* in 1929 that *"Russia be consecrated to Her Immaculate Heart, by the Pope in union with all the Bishops of the world, in one specific day."*

Some people think that this was already done, but it is not true. Pope Pius XII, on his own initiative, consecrated the world to the Immaculate Heart of Mary on October 31, 1942. The same Pope, on July 7, 1952, consecrated the Russian people to the Immaculate Heart of Mary. Pope Paul VI, speaking to the Fathers of the Second Vatican Council on November 21, 1964, again consecrated Russia to the Immaculate Heart of Mary.

These are *private* consecrations, not done according to Mary's wishes "in union with all the Bishops of the world."

So, when will the *REAL* consecration take place, according to the *exact* information of Sr. Marie (Lucia) of the Sorrows? Only God knows! It seems that there is a strange, unexplainable opposition to this Universal act. Surely the devil and the Russian propaganda have something to do about it. Or, perhaps we are not ready yet for such a salvific and extraordinary consecration. Maybe this act would be accomplished only by a greater and general devotion to both her Immaculate Heart, through the daily Rosary, and the Five First Saturdays.

A PRAYER FOR PEACE IN THE WORLD AND THE CONVERSION OF RUSSIA

Queen of the Rosary, sweet Virgin of Fatima, who was pleased to appear in the land of Portugal and bring peace, both interior and exterior, to that once so troubled country, we beg of you to watch over our own country and to assure its moral and spiritual revival. We beg you, O Mary, Queen of all the nations of the world, give us the conversion of Russia and preserve us from the dangers of Communism. Bring back peace to all the nations of the world, so that all, and our own nation in particular, may be happy to call you their Queen and the Queen of Peace. But there will not be a real peace in the world unless Russia is converted. We beseech you, therefore, O Lady of the Rosary of Fatima, and our Sweet Mother and Queen, obtain for all humanity the conversion of Russia and a lasting peace. Amen.

PART THREE —
OUR DEVOTION TO MARY

THAT MARY MAY LIVE IN ME

The following chapter is a summary of the Mariology of Venerable James Alberione (1884-1971), the founder of the Society of St. Paul (Priests and Brothers), of the Daughters of St. Paul and three other Congregations of women, and of four Secular Institutes, which constitute the "Pauline Family."

I was very fortunate to live with the Rev. Alberione from 1922 to 1936, when I left for the United States of America; he was, in fact, my confessor and spiritual director. I can truthfully testify of his profound and sincere devotion to Mary. It seems, for him, that everything depended, after God, on Mary, the Mother of God, the Mother of the Church, our Mother and the Queen of the Apostles. This is why he could accomplish so much at the service of the Church and the People of God, through the media of social communications.

Devotion to Mary is the fragrance of our faith, the heavenly smile to the faithful, the note of joy in our hearts, the dearest throb of our Christian life.

1. REASONS FOR DEVOTION TO MARY. — The first reason for devotion is love, and therefore, for the same reasons we love Mary, we also are devoted to her.

These reasons can be reduced to seven:

a) **God's special love for her.** "God loves the Virgin alone more than all the other Saints together," writes Father Suarez. St. Bonaventure, St. Anselm, St. Augustine and others affirm the same thing. Our Lady is so greatly loved by God because she is the most beautiful creature, both in the natural and the supernatural order: "I came out of the mouth of the most High, the firstborn before all creatures" (Ecclus 24:5).

b) **Her dignity.** God can create a firmament that is richer with stars, a more immense ocean, a more fertile land, but He cannot create a greater Mother, for there cannot possibly be a mother greater than she who calls God Himself her Son. From this great honor of divine Motherhood, as from the inexhaustible source, immense treasures flow to Mary.

c) **Mary's sanctity.** Willing His Mother to be the most loved and most honored of all creatures, God made her the most worthy of love and honor. Thus He enriched her with more graces than all the Angels and Saints together.

d) **The devotion that the Church has had to Mary through every century.**

e) **The benefits obtained through her intercession.**

f) **The love she bears us.**

g) **The sign of eternal predestination that this devotion brings us.**

Whoever avoids Mary encounters death; whoever finds Mary finds life.

2. QUALITIES OF TRUE DEVOTION. — It must be **interior, tender, holy, constant,** and **unselfish.**

Interior: that is, it must begin from our heart and must stem from our esteem for Mary and from our knowledge of her greatness.

Tender: that is, it must be full of confidence. The soul must have recourse to Mary as to a good and true mother in all its needs with great simplicity, trust and tenderness — in doubts, to be enlightened; in temptations, to be sustained; in weakness, to be strengthened; in falls, to be uplifted; in discouragement, to be encouraged; in scruples, to be freed from them; in crosses and adversites, to be consoled.

Holy: that is, it must lead the soul to avoid sin and imitate Mary's virtues, especially her profound humility, obedience, faith, constant prayer, purity, ardent charity, heroic patience and angelic sweetness.

Constant: that is, it must strengthen the soul in virtue and render it courageous in opposing the maxims of the world, the desires of the flesh, and the temptations of the devil.

Unselfish: that is, it must lead the soul to seek God alone rather than self.

A true devotee of Mary does not serve this august Queen because of self-interest but simply because Mary deserves to be served. He does not love her because he hopes to receive favors but because she is amiable. Thus a devotee loves and serves Mary faithfully in aridity as well as in times of sweetness and sensible consolations.

How dear to God and His Blessed Mother is such a devoted soul!

3. FOUNDATION OF TRUE DEVOTION TO MARY.
— Devotion to Mary has its foundations in God, in Jesus Christ, in the Church, in Mary herself, and in the Liturgy.

In God: Mary was in the thought and will of God from all eternity: "I was set up from eternity" (Prov 8:23). In the terrestrial paradise God promised our fallen first parents a Woman who would crush the devil's head: the Woman was Mary. God inspired the prophets to speak of her, of her privileges and her gifts. He raised up magnanimous women to prefigure her. He preserved her from original sin from the first instant of her conception. He filled her with graces. He associated her with the work of Redemption and crowned her life with her glorious Assumption into Heaven.

In Jesus Christ: for Mary lived, worked, and prayed with Him, and with Him she shared the joys and sorrows of family life. As the Redeemer, he willed her to be Co-redemptrix.

In the Church: which was founded beneath Mary's gaze, and which, with her help, began to spread. The Church invoked Jesus and Mary with the same hope and always united Mary's amiable feasts to the majestic feasts of Jesus.

In Mary herself: Because of her mission and virtues Mary deserves our respect, our confidence, our love and our devotion. The greatness of her Divine Son Jesus reflects such a resplendent light of nobility and sublimity on her that one cannot help venerating and loving her.

Lastly, devotion to Mary also has a **liturgical** basis. The Liturgy, even the most ancient, favors Marian devotion. In the Liturgy attributed to St. James we read: "Let us commemorate the Holy, Immaculate, most glorious and blessed Mary our Lady, Mother of our God and ever Virgin."

The Liturgy of St. John Chrysostom says: "Let us commemorate the most holy, most pure and most blessed of all creatures, Mary, our glorious Lady, Mother of God, ever Virgin." In the most ancient Liturgy of the Ethiopians we find these words: "Rejoice, O Virgin, always; at all times offer our prayers to God so that our sins may be forgiven; intercede at the throne of your Son, so that He may have compassion on our souls." Finally the Blessed Virgin is commemorated in the Latin liturgy so that she may obtain protection and help from God for all the faithful.

Thus Mary has every right to our devotion, love and veneration; let us respond generously.

In the sublime canticle of the Magnificat, Mary says that the time will come when all nations "shall call me blessed" (Luke 1:48). With these words she announces and predicts her greatness, and this prophecy is admirably fulfilled throughout the ages. The venerated name of the great Mother of God echoes gloriously everywhere, in civilized as well as in uncivilized countries!

May your devotion, O Mary, grow, increase and expand as long as there are men on earth and Angels in Heaven! As long as God will be God! But it most assuredly will be like this and I shall ever rejoice, O my Mother, for you are worthy of every praise. Obtain for me the grace that I may honor, love, beseech and imitate you on earth so that I may be able to enjoy your company in Heaven forever.

Long live Mary, her name, devotion and love!

Let us resolve to pray to the Blessed virgin especially with the recitation of the Rosary. Mary will reign in our hearts and if Mary is with us, what can we fear? With Mary's love in our heart we shall attain eternal salvation.

A Thought from St. Bernard: *Let us try to venerate this divine Mother Mary with all the affections of our heart, for it is God's will that we receive every grace through Mary's hands.*

OUR "GREAT LOVE" MARY

My "Greatest Love," naturally is God; as He will always be, here on earth, and, I hope, in Heaven, for all eternity. God has always been good to me, even though I offended Him many times.

In His mercy, God called me, at the age of eleven, to the religious and priestly life, I served Him, although imperfectly, for 56 years as a professed religious, and 52 years as a priest. I am only sorry that my love and my service were not as perfect as they should have been.

My second Great Love was and will always be Mary, who saved me from certain drowning at the age of ten. While going down for the third time, to the bottom of the river Po in Piedmont, Italy, completely exhausted, the thought of the Lady of Lourdes, all dressed in white, with a blue sash, and golden roses on her feet, was in my mind and in my prayer, until my older brother Louis saw me, jumped into the water and saved me.

My mother had her own way of expressing her devotion to Mary. I remember that, during big and devastating storms, she went upstairs, lit candles in front of a statue of Mary and said the Rosary. On those occasions, I knelt down with her, and looked at the beautiful statue of Mary.

My godmother, Maria, was a truly saintly woman. She was the one who taught me how to honor Mary by bringing her flowers from the garden, removing my hat when passing in front of an image of the Blessed Virgin, making a Sign of the Cross and saying the Hail Mary.

During the months of May and October, the girls and the women of my town used to get together at the little shrine at the crossroad, to recite the Rosary and the Litanies of the Blessed Virgin. I always admired them and I joined them at a distance, because men were not accustomed to pray or be seen praying with women.

I loved the processions when the people carried the statue of Mary along the decorated streets of my town, saying the Rosary and singing hymns, and finally gathering at the church for the concluding Benediction of the Most Blessed Sacrament. Even though I was a very young boy, I never missed these processions. I am sure that it was Mary who inspired my vocation.

Visiting historical shrines dedicated to Our Lady, usually built on high hills or mountains in Italy, was always a great event in my life.

But I always admired the little outdoor shrines at the crossroads, where people could stop and say the Hail Mary. I myself built a little niche in the front wall of the house where I was born, and much later on, in 1975, I rebuilt an abandoned outdoor shrine at our Mother House in New York. To see Our Lady honored was always in my blood.

When I entered the Society of St. Paul at the city of Alba (Italy), in 1922, at the age of eleven, what struck me most was the devotion to Mary encouraged by the founder, Rev. James Alberione. ''Be devoted to Mary Immaculate,'' he used to say, ''pray to her every day, perform little acts of devotion or mortification to please her, try to imitate her virtues, and do not forget the practice of the 'Three Hail Marys.' When you get up in the morning, and when you go to sleep at night.''

A few days after I was ordained a priest, August 15, 1936, I was invited to join a parish pilgrimage to the historical old Shrine of Our Lady of Crea, built on top of a high hill in the wine growing region of Monferrato, Italy. On that day I consecrated my life and my work as a priest to Mary, Queen of the Apostles. Twenty five years later, in 1961, on the occasion of my Silver Jubilee of the priesthood, I visited another famous shrine, not far away from the town of my birth, that of Our Lady of Oropa, built on top of a mountain. That day I admired the rebuilt shrine, shining in the blue of the sky, while thick clouds below covered the surroundings. What a sight! And what an occasion to thank Mary for 25 years in the priesthood.

Also in 1961, I visited and prayed at the basilicas of Our Lady of Fatima in Portugal, and Our Lady of Lourdes in France. I am unable to describe the feelings and the spiritual pleasure I felt during these two visits!

Finally, by the grace of God and the continuous protection of the Blessed Virgin Mary, in 1986, I celebrated in Rome, at the magnificent shrine of Mary, Queen of the Apostles, my Golden Jubilee of Priesthood. What an occasion to thank again God and my sweet Mother Mary!

The day after the celebration in Rome, I went on a pilgrimage to the Holy Land, where I had the opportunity to pray and celebrate Mass at the Church of the Cenacle where Mary received the Holy Spirit with the Apostles, and where, it is believed, she died and was assumed into heaven. I was privileged to visit and celebrate Mass at the the magnificent basilica built over the place where Mary lived with Jesus and Joseph at Nazareth in Galilee. Also, I visited Mt. Carmel, and prayed in the first church dedicated to the future Mother of God.

* * *

In our spiritual life, the Eucharist, the Bread of life, is unquestionably the fundamental element of sanctification and of the worship of God. The Word of God, given to us through the Magisterium of the Church, is an essential part of the intellectual formation of the People of God. In my own opinion, prayer and devotion to Mary will complete our formation and establish the Kingdom of God in our soul.

Mary, my sweet Mother, I love and thank you! You always protected me in numerous physical dangers; you helped me overcome many temptations; you guided me in my spiritual life; and especially, you obtained for me, from God, many graces and blessings. With you I want to live; with your special assistance I want to die; and with God and you I want to spend my eternity in heaven!

Now, what about you? Do you love Mary, at least a little? Try and see, and you will realize how sweet it is to love and honor such a wonderful Mother, and how many graces and blessings you will receive from God, through her powerful intercession. You do not have to do much to please her; select from this book the devotion or the prayer you like most, and follow it every day.

St. John Berchmans, a young Jesuit saint, declared: "It does not matter what you do to honor Mary; it could be the smallest and the most insignificant thing, but do it CONSTANTLY."

— Rev. Joseph A. Viano, S.S.P.

CONCLUSION:

A DECLARATION OF LOVE TO MARY

When Jesus on the Cross pronounced the words: "It is consummated" (John 19:30), the world was redeemed and saved, heavenly wrath was appeased, Heaven was opened anew, and we regained the right to our celestial heritage. But that which is important to note and which proves the necessity of devotion to Mary for salvation is the fact that Jesus announced to the world that all was accomplished, after having said to Mary, indicating John to her: "Behold you son," and to the beloved disciple, indicating Mary to him: "Behold your Mother" (John 19:26-27). The Divine Redeemer declared that nothing more remained to be done only after He had given us Mary as our Mother. Devotion to the Virgin, is, therefore, willed by Jesus and is necessary for salvation.

Mary is the tree of life for souls who press close to her. Blessed are they who hold tight to her always! "He that shall find me, shall find life, and shall have salvation from the Lord" (Prov. 8:35).

O Immaculate Virgin, you let us understand that whoever tries to know you and to make you known will have eternal life as a reward: "They that explain me shall have life everlasting" (Eccles. 24:31). Therefore, I shall do my utmost to know you, to honor you, to pray to you, to love you, and to imitate you. I shall not spare any effort or study in order to make known your virtues, your merits, and your mercy; I shall do my best to propagate devotion to you and to make you known, loved, and imitated.

Oh, if I could only lead the entire world to your feet! I want to live and die in your arms, close to your motherly Heart. I want to love you with all the strength of my soul, so that after pronouncing your most dear name for the last time here below, I may go to enjoy you forever in Heaven. Virgin Mary, Mother of Jesus, make us saints! Queen of all Saints, pray for us!